Nita Mehta's
QUICK
Vegetarian Cooking

Nita Mehta

M.Sc. (Food and Nutrition), Gold Medalist

CO AUTHOR
TANYA MEHTA

SNAB
Publishers Pvt. Ltd.

Nita Mehta's
QUICK
Vegetarian Cooking

First Edition 2002

ISBN 81-7869-026-5

Food Styling & Photography: **SNAB**

Layout and laser typesetting:

National Information Technology Academy
3A/3, Asaf Ali Road
New Delhi-110002
☎ 3252948

Published by:

Publishers Pvt Ltd
3A/3 Asaf Ali Road
New Delhi-110002

The Best of Cookery Books

Editorial and Marketing office:
E-348, Greater Kailash-II, N.Delhi-48
Fax: 91-11-6235218 *Tel:* 91-11-6214011, 6238727
E-Mail: nitamehta@email.com
snab@snabindia.com
Website: http://www.nitamehta.com
Website: http://www.snabindia.com

Printed at:
THOMSON PRESS (INDIA) LIMITED

Distributed by:
THE VARIETY BOOK DEPOT
A.V.G. Bhavan, M 3 Con Circus
New Delhi - 110 001
Tel: 3327175, 3322567; Fax: 3714335

Price: Rs.189/-

Picture on page 1:	**Pasta with Mushrooms & Tomatoes**
	Quick Tiramisu
Picture on page 2:	**Vegetable au Gratin**
Picture on cover:	**Kandhari Khumb**
	Tandoori Chaat
Picture on back cover:	**Naaza**
Picture on last page:	**Chocolate Desire**
	Stuffed Cheese Steaks with Salsa

Introduction

Here's a Vegetarian Gourmet's delight – vegetarian recipes at their best and yet quick and simple to prepare. The cooking method is very simple to get the food ready at a short notice. The spices are added to perk up the vegetarian food, converting them into a real gastronomer's delight. Do not let the long list of ingredients in some of the recipes, scare you! Though the number of ingredients may be a bit too long, they are all likely to be available in your kitchen.

Tandoori food is quick and simple to serve. You may hesitate to start making tandoori food in your oven. Therefore, to make you confident, I have given some very useful tips in the beginning. Keep them in mind while using your oven for tandoori items. Your friends and family can now look forward to delicious *Tandoori Chaat* or the pickle flavoured *Achaari Paneer Tikka*. The desserts are wonderful to look at and good to eat! They have been twisted and turned to make them simple and quick to prepare. The Italian favourite *Tiramisu* has chocolate chip biscuits instead of the sponge cake and cheese spread instead of cream cheese. The quick fix dessert of ice cream, pastries and some tinned fruit churns out a wonderful *ice cream trifle*. The delicious Indian recipes like *Manzil-e-Paneer* and *Kandhari Khumb* are sure to be great hits! Pasta has become very popular. A separate section includes pasta recipes. The baked dishes too are very different from the usual. The *Bread & Cheese Bake* turns out excellent. All it takes is a few slices of bread and some cheese to churn out a deliciously exciting dish. *Sweet and Sour Cabbage* and *Italian Tomatoes* are baked with tomato based sauces and are a welcome change from the bakes cooked in white sauce.

Enjoy preparing "Quick Vegetarian Recipes" and surprise your guests with exotic different vegetarian meals.

Nita Mehta

Contents

INDIAN - DRY & MASALA 58

BAKED DISHES 75

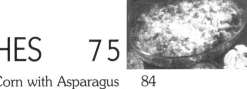

PASTA & CONTINENTAL DISHES 92

RICE & BREADS   104

DESSERTS   116

TANDOORI TIKKAS & KEBABS

STRAIGHT FROM YOUR OVEN

Tips for Perfect Barbecuing

- Always keep the food to be barbecued or grilled on a wire rack and never on a tray. There is always a little liquid/water that comes out during grilling/barbecuing and if the food is on a tray then it collects around the food. This prevents the food from getting crisp on the outside. Whereas, if the food is placed on a wire rack, the water or liquid falls down and lets the food get crisp.
- Add a little cornflour or besan (gramflour) or cheese to the marinade so that the marinade sticks well to the vegetable and does not fall off while grilling.
- Add a little oil or melted butter to the marinade. It keeps the food succulent and soft from inside.
- Basting the food in between grilling is important to prevent it from turning dry. To baste, pour some melted butter or oil on the food in the oven after it is half done and then grill further.
- Do not cut vegetables into very small pieces. If they are small, they slip off from the grill. Cut them according to the space inbetween the wires of the oven grill.
- If the distance between the wires of the rack is too wide, and there is a chance of your piece falling below the rack then cover the wire rack with well greased silver foil and place the vegetables on it.
- Cover the plate beneath the grill with aluminium foil to collect the drippings of the marinade. This makes the cleaning very simple.
- Rub oil generously on the wire rack of the oven on which the vegetables are going to be placed. If you do not do so, the coating of the grilled vegetables generally tends to stick to the grill and comes off from the vegetables when you pick up the ready food from the grill.
- When you use skewers for grilling, remove the wire rack of the oven or tandoor. The skewers should not touch anything, because it then becomes difficult to remove the kebabs from the skewers after they are done.
- Never over grill or keep food for too long in the oven. Paneer and other vegetables tend to become hard on doing so.
- Marinate well in advance and keep in the refrigerator. Grill before serving time. If the food is grilled to much in advance, it does not remain too soft.
- Remember to preheat the oven before you start grilling.

Makai Mirch

Mozzarella cheese holds the filling of diced paneer and corn together, because on cooking the cheese melts, binding the two together.

Picture on facing page   *Serves 4*

4 medium size capsicums

MARINADE
2 tbsp lemon juice, 1 tsp ginger paste, ½ tsp garlic paste, 1 tbsp oil, ¾ tsp salt

STUFFING
100 gm paneer - finely cut into ¼" cubes (1 cup)
½ cup grated mozzarella cheese
½ cup corn kernels - tinned or freshly boiled
1 tbsp green coriander - chopped
2 tbsp oil
¼ tsp hing (asafoetida), 1 tsp jeera (cumin seeds) and ½ tsp sarson (mustard seeds)
1 small onion - cut into half and then into rings, to get shredded onion
4-5 cashews - crushed on a chakla-belan (rolling board & pin), 8-10 kishmish
½ tsp red chilli powder, ¾ tsp salt, ½ tsp garam masala, ¼ tsp amchoor

BASTING
2 tbsp oil or butter

1. Cut a slice from the top of each capsicum. Scoop out the center with the help of a knife. Mix all the ingredients of the marinade and rub liberally on the inside of the capsicums. Cover with caps and leave aside for ½ hour.
2. Take a heavy bottom kadhai and heat oil. Put in the hing, jeera, and sarson. Wait till jeera turns golden.
3. Add onions and cook till soft. Add cashews and kishmish. Stir. Add red chilli powder, salt, garam masala and amchoor.
4. Add corn and cook for 1 minute. Add paneer and mix well. Remove from fire. Add mozzarella cheese. Mix. Keep filling aside.
5. Stuff the capsicums with this filling. They should be stuffed well but not to bursting point. Rub oil on the stuffed capsicums. Cover with the caps and secure them with wooden tooth-picks.
6. Oil and wipe the skewers. Skewer the capsicums. Small onions or pieces of potatoes can be used inbetween to prevent them from slipping. Put the skewers into the gas tandoor or oven and cook for 10 minutes or till they turn blackish at some places. Turn 1-2 times inbetween to grill evenly. Serve.

Tandoori Bharwaan Aloo : Recipe on page 13, Makai Mirch ➢

Baby Corn Bullets

Enjoy it rolled up in roomali rotis with some onion slices mixed with hari chutney!

Serves 4-5

200 gm thick baby corns - keep whole
juice of ½ lemon
1-2 capsicums - cut into large 1" pieces
8 cherry tomatoes or 1 large tomato - cut into 8 pieces & pulp removed
1 onion - cut into fours & separated or 4 spring onions (keep white part whole)
1-2 tbsp melted butter for basting
some chaat masala - to sprinkle

MARINADE
1½ cups thick curd - hang for 30 minutes
2 tsp cornflour
2 tbsp thick cream or malai
¼ tsp ajwain (carom seeds)
1 tbsp thick ginger-garlic paste (squeeze out the liquid)
½ tsp kala namak (black salt), ¼ tsp haldi
1 tbsp tandoori masala, ¼ tsp red chilli powder, ¾ tsp salt

1. Boil 4-5 cups water with 2 tsp salt, ¼ tsp haldi and juice of ½ lemon. Add baby corns to boiling water. After the boil returns, boil for 1 minute or till slightly soft. Strain and wipe dry the corns on a clean kitchen towel. Keep aside.
2. Mix all ingredients of the marinade in a large bowl.
3. Rub oil generously on a wire rack or grill of the oven.
4. Add baby corns first to the marinade in the bowl and mix well to coat the marinade. Remove from bowl and arrange on the greased rack. In the remaining marinade in the bowl, add onion, capsicum and tomatoes. Leave these in the bowl itself. Marinate all for atleast ½ hour.
5. Grill baby corns first in an oven at 200°C for 15 minutes or roast in a gas tandoor. Pour a little melted butter on them. Put the onion and capsicum also along with the corns and grill for 10 minutes. Lastly put the tomatoes in the oven with the onion-capsicum and grill further for 2-3 minutes.
6. Serve sprinkled with some chat masala, alongwith lemon wedges.

Tandoori Bharwaan Aloo

Serves 6   *Picture on page 11*

3 big (longish) potatoes
some chaat masala to sprinkle

FILLING

3 almonds - crushed with a belan (rolling pin), 4 tbsp grated paneer (50 gm)
1 tbsp poodina (mint) leaves - chopped, 1 green chilli - deseeded and chopped
¼ tsp garam masala, ¼ tsp red chilli powder, ¼ tsp salt, a pinch amchoor

COVERING

½ cup thick curd - hang in a muslin cloth for 30 minutes
1 tbsp ginger paste
¼ tsp red chilli powder, ¾ tsp salt, ¼ tsp orange tandoori colour or haldi

CRUSH TOGETHER TO A ROUGH POWDER

1 tsp shah jeera (black cumin), seeds of 2 moti illaichi (brown cardamom)
2-3 blades of javitri (mace), 6-8 saboot kali mirch (peppercorns)

1. Boil potatoes in salted water till just tender. When they are no longer hot, peel skin.
2. Mix crushed almonds with mint leaves, green chillies, 4 tbsp grated paneer, ¼ tsp salt, ¼ tsp garam masala, ¼ tsp red chilli and a pinch of amchoor.
3. Grind or crush shah jeera, seeds of moti illaichi, peppercorns, and 2-3 pinches of javitri to a coarse powder.
4. To the paneer mixture, add ¼-½ teaspoon of the above freshly ground spice powder also. Keep the leftover powder aside.
5. Mix hung curd, ginger paste, the left over freshly ground powder and red chilli powder and salt. Add haldi or orange colour.
6. Run the tip of a fork on the surface of the potatoes, making the surface rough. (The rough surface holds the masalas well).
7. Cut each potato into 2 halves, vertically. Scoop out, just a little, to get a small cavity in each potato with the back of a teaspoon. Stuff with paneer filling.
8. With a spoon apply the curd mixture on the outside (backside) of the potatoes and on the rim also (not on the filling).
9. Grill potatoes in a gas tandoor or a preheated oven at 210°C/410°F for 15 minutes on a greased wire rack till they get slightly dry.
10. Spoon some oil or melted butter on them (baste) and then grill further for 10 minutes till the coating turns absolutely dry. Sprinkle some chaat masala and serve hot.

Malai Khumb

Serves 6-8

200 gm mushrooms - choose big ones
juice of ½ lemon
1 tbsp butter - melted, for basting
chaat masala to sprinkle

MARINADE
4 tbsp thick cream
1 cup thick curd - hang in a muslin cloth for 15 minutes
2-4 tbsp grated cheese, preferably mozzarella
2 tbsp oil
1 tbsp cornflour
1 tbsp ginger paste
¾ tsp salt
2 tbsp chopped coriander

1. Wash mushrooms well. Trim the stalks neatly.
2. Boil 4-5 cups water with 1 tsp salt and juice of ½ lemon. As soon as the boil comes, add the mushrooms. Let them boil for a minute. Strain and pat dry them on a clean kitchen towel.
3. Squeeze curd and transfer to a bowl. Mix cream, cheese, oil, cornflour, ginger paste, salt and coriander to the hung curd.
4. Marinate the mushrooms in the curd mixture till serving time.
5. To serve, preheat the oven to 180°C. Arrange the marinated mushrooms on a greased wire rack with head side up. Pat the left over marinade on the mushroom heads. You can arrange these on thin skewers also. Grill in a hot oven at 180°C for 15-20 minutes till the coating turns dry.
6. Melt some butter. In between, pour some melted butter on the mushrooms.
7. Sprinkle chaat masala. Serve with mint chutney mixed with a little hung curd. Garnish with onion rings.

Tandoori Hari Gobhi

Serves 12

**500 gm (2 medium heads) broccoli - cut into medium sized florets with small stalks
chaat masala and lemon wedges**

MARINADE
1 cup thick curd - hang for 15 minutes or more and squeeze to remove all water
1 tbsp kasoori methi (dry fenugreek leaves)
**1 tbsp besan (gram flour) - dry roasted on a tawa (griddle) on low heat till fragrant,
for about 1 minute**
1 tbsp oil
1 tbsp ginger-garlic paste
½ tsp red chilli powder
¼ tsp haldi
1 tsp salt
¼ tsp kala namak (black salt)
1 tsp tandoori masala

1. Boil 5-6 cups of water in a large pan. Add 2 tsp salt and 1 tsp sugar to the water. Add broccoli pieces to the boiling water. After the boil returns, remove from fire. Leave in hot water for 10-15 minutes. Drain. Refresh with cold water. Strain. Wipe the pieces well with a clean kitchen towel till well dried.
2. Mix all the ingredients of the marinade in a large pan. Add the broccoli to it and mix well. Keep in the refrigerator till the time of serving.
3. To serve, rub the grill of the oven or tandoor with some oil. Place the broccoli on it. Grill for 10-15 minutes. Do not over grill it, it turns too dry.
4. Serve hot sprinkled with chaat masala and lemon wedges.

Achaari Paneer Tikka

Pickle flavoured masala paneer tikka.

Makes 16

400 gms paneer - cut into 1½" rectangles of ¾" thickness
2 tsp ginger-garlic paste
1 tsp cornflour
1 cup curd - hang in a muslin cloth for ½ hour
2 tbsp oil
½ tsp haldi (turmeric) powder, 1 tsp amchoor (dried mango powder)
1 tsp dhania powder, ½ tsp garam masala, 1 tsp salt or to taste, ½ tsp sugar
1 onion - chopped finely, 2 green chillies - chopped
some chaat masala to sprinkle

ACHAARI MASALA
1 tbsp saunf (aniseeds)
½ tsp rai (mustard seeds)
a pinch of methi daana (fenugreek seeds)
½ tsp kalonji (onion seeds)
½ tsp jeera (cumin seeds)

1. Cut paneer into 1½" rectangles, of about ¾" thickness.
2. Collect seeds of achaari masala- saunf, rai, methi daana, kalonji & jeera together.
3. Heat 2 tbsp oil. Add the collected seeds together to the hot oil. Let saunf change colour.
4. Add onions and chopped green chillies. Cook till onions turn golden brown.
5. Reduce heat. Add haldi, amchoor, dhania powder, garam masala, salt and sugar. Mix. Remove from fire.
6. Beat curd till smooth. Add garlic-ginger paste and cornflour. Add the onion masala also to the curd.
7. Add the paneer cubes to the curd. Marinate till serving time.
8. At serving time, rub oil generously over the grill of the oven or wire rack of a gas tandoor. Place paneer on the greased wire rack or grill of the oven.
9. Heat an oven to 180°C or a gas tandoor on moderate flame. Grill paneer for 15 minutes. Spoon some oil or melted butter on the paneer pieces in the oven or tandoor and grill further for 5 minutes. Serve hot sprinkled with chaat masala.

Note: To cook the tikkas in the oven, place a drip tray under the wire rack on which the tikkas are placed, to collect the drippings.

Hare Chhole Ke Kebab

There are unlimited combinations for making vegetable kebabs, here hare chhole has been used to churn out deliciously succulent kebabs.

Makes 14

2 cups fresh green gram (hare chholia)
½ cup besan (gramflour) - roasted on a tawa for 1 minute, or till fragrant
2 slices bread - broken into pieces and churned in a mixer to get fresh crumbs
1 cup yogurt- hang in a muslin cloth for 30 minutes
1 small onion - chopped
1 tbsp ginger-garlic paste
3-4 green chillies - chopped
10 -12 fresh curry leaves
1 tbsp tandoori masala
1 tsp salt or to taste
1 tsp jeera
3 tbsp oil + oil for shallow frying
2-3 tbsp maida (plain flour)

CRUSH TOGETHER
1 tbsp saboot dhania (coriander seeds), 1 tsp roasted jeera (bhuna jeera)
½ tsp saboot kali mirch (black peppercorns)

1. Crush saboot dhania, bhuna jeera and saboot kali mirch on a chakla-belan (rolling board-pin).
2. Clean, wash hare chholia. Pressure cook hare chhole with the above crushed spices, ½ tsp salt and 1 cup water. Give one whistle. Remove from fire and keep aside. After the pressure drops down, mash the hot hare chholia with a potato masher or a karchhi. If there is any water, mash and dry the chholia on fire. Remove from fire.
3. Heat 3 tbsp oil, add jeera, let it change colour. Add chopped onion, ginger-garlic paste, chopped green chillies and curry leaves. Cook till onions turn light brown.
4. Add mashed chholia, pepper, salt, roasted besan, tandoori masala and hung yogurt. Cook for 5 minutes or till dry. Remove from fire. Cool.
5. Add bread crumbs and mix well.
6. Make marble sized balls of the chholia mixture. Flatten to form a kebab of about 2" diameter.
7. Roll in maida and shallow fry 3-4 pieces at a time on a hot tawa in 6 tbsp oil. Turn sides till both sides are crisp. Remove the kebabs on paper napkins. Serve.

Tandoori Phool

Serves 4-6

1 medium size gobi (cauliflower) - wash and keep whole with 1-2" stalk

MARINADE
¾ cup thick curd - hang for ½ hour
¼ cup thick cream or malai
1 tbsp oil
2 tbsp besan - roasted on a tawa for 1 minute or till fragrant
½ tbsp ginger paste
2 tsp tandoori masala
4-6 saboot kali mirch (black peppercorns) - crushed
½ tsp red chilli powder, ¼ tsp haldi
1 tsp salt

TO SERVE
2 onions - cut into fine rings, 2 tbsp finely chopped coriander
½ tsp chaat masala, 1 tomato - cut into slices

1. Boil 4 cups water with 1 tsp salt.
2. Add cauliflower. When the water starts to boil again, remove from fire. Let the cauliflower be in hot water for 3-4 minutes. Remove from water and keep aside.
3. Wipe the cauliflower with a clean kitchen towel. Keep aside.
4. Mix together in a bowl all ingredients of the marinade. Insert the marinade inside the cauliflower florets, from the bottom also. Rub the top with the left over marinade. Keep aside for atleast 1 hour.
5. Brush the grilling rack of the oven generously with oil. Place the marinated cauliflower on the greased grilling rack.
6. Grill in a hot oven at 200°C for 30 minutes or more till brown specs appear on the cauliflower. Keep aside till serving time.
7. To serve, cut the whole cauliflower into 4 big pieces right through the stalk. Cut each piece further into 2 pieces. Sprinkle chaat masala.
8. Add fresh coriander and chaat masala to the onions.
9. To serve, heat gobi in an oven or microwave till really hot. Arrange the pieces neatly in a serving platter. Sprinkle lemon juice. Garnish with onion rings, tomato slices, lemon wedges and mint sprigs.

Haryali Paneer Tikka

Serves 6

400 gm paneer - cut into 1½" long pieces, 1" thick
4 tbsp besan (gram flour)
1 tsp salt
4 tbsp oil

GRIND TO A FINE PASTE (CHUTNEY)
1 cup fresh hara dhania (green coriander)
2 tsp saunf (fennel)
5-6 flakes garlic
1" piece ginger
4 tbsp lemon juice
½ tsp salt

1. Grind together dhania, saunf, ginger, garlic, lemon juice and salt to a fine paste.
2. Slit the paneer pieces and keep aside.
3. Divide the chutney into 2 parts.
4. With one part of the chutney, stuff some chutney in the slits of all the paneer pieces. Keep the stuffed paneer aside.
5. Mix together the left over chutney, besan, salt and oil. Rub this all over the stuffed paneer pieces.
6. Rub oil generously over the grill of the oven or wire rack of a gas tandoor. Place paneer on the greased wire rack or grill of the oven or skewer the pieces.
7. Heat an oven to 180°C or a gas tandoor on moderate flame. Grill paneer for 15 minutes. Spoon some drops of oil on the paneer pieces in the oven or tandoor and grill further for 5 minutes. Serve hot.

Note: To cook the tikkas in the oven, place a drip tray covered with aluminium foil under the wire rack on which the tikkas are placed, to collect the drippings.

Tandoori Platter with Barbecue Sauce

The platter looks equally appetizing without the wooden skewers!

Picture on facing page   *Serves 8*

250 gm paneer - cut into large (1½") cubes, 2 capsicums - cut into large cubes
8 cherry tomatoes or 1 large tomato - cut into 8 pieces & pulp removed
200 gm (10-12) mushrooms - trim ends of the stalks, leaving them whole
100 gm baby corns - blanched with a pinch of haldi and 1 tsp salt in 3 cups water
1 onion - cut into fours & separated

MARINADE
1 cup thick curd - hang for 30 minutes, 2 tbsp thick cream, 2 tbsp oil
1 tbsp cornflour, 1 tbsp thick ginger-garlic paste
½ tsp black salt, ¼ tsp haldi or tandoori colour
2 tsp tandoori masala, ½ tsp red chilli powder, ¾ tsp salt or to taste

BARBECUE SAUCE
3 tbsp butter, 4-5 flakes garlic - crushed
2 large tomatoes - pureed till smooth
¼ cup ready made tomato puree
¼ tsp red chilli powder, ½ tsp pepper
¾ tsp salt or to taste, ¼ tsp sugar, ½ tsp worcestershire sauce, ½ tsp soya sauce

1. Rub oil generously on a wire rack or grill of the oven.
2. Mix all ingredients of the marinade. Add paneer, mushrooms and baby corns to the marinade and mix well to coat the marinade. Remove from bowl and arrange on the rack or on greased wooden skewers. In the remaining marinade which is sticking to the sides of the bowl, add onion, capsicum and tomatoes. Leave these in the bowl itself. Marinate all for atleast ½ hour.
3. Grill paneer and vegetables in the oven at 210°C/410°F for 12-15 minutes or roast in a gas tandoor, on the wire rack or on skewers. Spoon a little oil/melted butter (basting) on them. Add onion, capsicum and tomatoes. Grill for another 5-7 minutes.
4. For the barbecue sauce, heat oil in a kadhai. Add garlic and cook till light brown. Add tomatoes, tomato puree and red chilli powder. Cook for 5 minutes till well blended. Add all other ingredients and ½ cup water to get a thin sauce. Boil. Simmer for 2 minutes. Remove from fire and keep aside.
5. To serve, put some hot sauce on the serving plate. Arrange grilled vegetables on the sauce with or without skewers. Pour some hot sauce over the vegetables. Serve at once. You may serve the platter on rice too.

Subz Kakori

Very soft and delicious vegetarian seekh kebabs.

Serves 4-5

3 potatoes (medium) - boiled
(250 gm) 2 cups jimikand (yam) - chopped and boiled
½ cup crumbled paneer
4 tbsp cashewnuts - ground
1 tsp ginger paste
1 tsp garlic paste
1 big onion - very finely chopped (1 cup)
2 green chillies - very finely chopped
2 tbsp green coriander - very finely chopped
1 tsp bhuna jeera (cumin roasted)
1 tsp red chilli powder, ¼ tsp amchoor
2 bread slices - crumbled in a grinder to get fresh crumbs
1½ tsp salt, or to taste
a pinch of tandoori red colour

BASTING
2 tbsp melted butter or oil

GARNISH
tandoori khatta masala or chaat masala

1. Boil the potatoes. Peel and mash.
2. Pressure cook chopped yam with ½ cup water and ½ tsp salt to give 3 whistles. Remove from fire. After the pressure drops, keep it on fire to dry, if there is any excess water. Mash it to a paste.
3. Mix mashed potatoes, yam and all other ingredients, making a slightly stiff dough.
4. Oil and wipe the skewers. Heat the gas tandoor or oven at 180°C. Remove the wire rack. Press into sausage-shaped kababs on the greased skewers and cook for about 5 minutes in a hot tandoor or grill. Pour some melted butter on the kebabs to baste them when they get half done. Turn side and grill for 5-7 minutes or till golden brown. If you do not wish to grill the kebabs, shallow fry in 2 tbsp oil in a pan on low heat, turning sides till browned evenly.
5. Sprinkle some tandoori or chaat masala and serve with onion rings and lemon wedges.

Note: Turn kebabs on the skewers only after they are half done, otherwise they tend to break.

Tandoori Chaat

Serves 4   *Picture on cover*

2 capsicums - deseeded and cut into 1½" pieces (preferably 1 green & 1 red capsicum)
200 gm paneer - cut into 1" cubes (8 pieces)
2 small onions - each cut into 4 pieces
4 fresh pineapple slices - each cut into 4 pieces (see note)
2 tomatoes - each cut into 4 pieces and pulp removed
1 tsp garam masala
2 tbsp lemon juice
1 tbsp tandoori masala or barbecue masala
2 tbsp oil
1 tsp salt, or to taste
1½ tsp chaat masala

1. Mix all the vegetables, pineapple and paneer in a bowl.
2. Sprinkle all the ingredients on them. Mix well.
3. Heat the greased grill or wire rack of the oven or tandoor at 180° C. First place the paneer, pineapple and onions only on the greased grill or rack. Grill for about 15 minutes, till the edges start to change colour.
4. After the paneer is almost done, put the capsicum and tomatoes also on the wire rack with the paneer etc. Grill for 10 minutes.
5. Remove from the oven straight to the serving plate. Sprinkle some chaat masala and lemon juice, if you like.

Note: If tinned pineapple is being used, grill it in the second batch with capsicum and tomatoes since it is already soft.

Hari Seekh Salad

An unusual, roasted green salad on skewers. Good to start the meal!

Serves 6

12 big spinach leaves
1 medium broccoli - broken into small florets
5 whole, white part of spring onions, choose big ones
12 cabbage leaves - separated

MARINADE
1¼ cups yoghurt - hang for ½ hour in a muslin cloth
1 onion - grind to a paste
1 tbsp freshly ground pepper
1 tsp garam masala, ½ tsp amchoor
1½ tbsp oil, 1¼ tsp salt

BASTING
left over marinade

1. Clean and wash all the vegetables. Pat dry the spinach and cabbage leaves on a clean kitchen towel.
2. Boil 4 cups water with 1 tsp salt and 1 tsp sugar. Add broccoli. Remove from fire. Let it be in hot water for 5 minutes. Drain and refresh in cold water. Wipe dry on a clean kitchen towel.
3. Mix all the ingredients of the marinade – yoghurt, onion paste, pepper, garam masala, amchoor, and 1½ tbsp oil.
4. Take one vegetable at a time and spread the marinade on each vegetable or leaf on both the sides thoroughly. Mix well, leave aside for 1 hour mixing atleast twice in between.
5. Oil and wipe the skewers. Heat the gas tandoor on moderate heat or the oven at 180°C.
6. Skewer the vegetables - thread them starting with broccoli, then fold a cabbage leaf and insert, fold a spinach leaf once and then fold again (like a pan) and insert, then insert a whole spring onion and then again another folded cabbage leaf and spinach leaf in the same skewer, repeating till the skewer gets fully covered (cabbage and spinach leaf have been threaded twice).
7. Spread the left over marinade on the skewered vegetables with hand.
8. Put the skewers in the tandoor or oven and cook for 2 minutes.
9. Take out the skewer carefully and baste them again with the marinade. Put them back into the tandoor or oven. Cook for 5 minutes. Serve hot.

Poodina Kaju Kebabs

Serves 6-8

2 big potatoes - chopped
2 small onions - chopped
¾ cup shelled peas
½ of a small cauliflower - cut into small florets
4 slices of bread - broken into pieces and ground in a mixer to get fresh crumbs
1" piece ginger - crushed
5-6 flakes garlic - crushed
½ tsp red chilli powder
½ tsp garam masala
2 tsp tomato sauce
1½ tsp salt or to taste
1 green chilli - finely chopped
2 tbsp chopped fresh coriander
15 cashewnuts - ground to a coarse powder in a small spice grinder
4 tbsp cornflour

FILLING
2-3 tbsp very finely chopped poodina
½ small onion - chopped finely
¼ tsp amchoor
¼ tsp salt

1. Pressure cook potatoes, cauliflower, onion and peas with 1 cup water to give 2 whistles. Keep on low fire for 5 minutes. Remove from fire. Cool. Drain and leave in a sieve for about 5 minutes to remove excess moisture.
2. Mash the vegetables and add ginger, garlic, red chilli powder, garam masala, salt and tomato sauce.
3. Add green chilli, fresh coriander, cashewnuts, cornflour and fresh bread crumbs.
4. Mix all ingredients of the filling together. Keep aside.
5. Break off small balls of the vegetable mixture and pat them into flat circular shapes about ½" thick, with wet hands.
6. Stuff a little of the filling and form a ball. Shape again into a flat disc.
7. Heat 4-5 tbsp oil in a frying pan or on a tawa and fry gently over medium heat, turning once.
8. Remove on a kitchen towel to remove excess oil.
9. Serve hot with poodina chutney.

Hara Bhara Kebab

Serves 8

1 cup channe ki dal (split gram)
1 bundle (600 gm) spinach - only leaves, chopped very finely
3 tbsp oil
3 slices bread - broken into pieces and churned in a mixer to get fresh crumbs
3 tbsp cornflour
2 green chillies - chopped finely
½ tsp red chilli powder, ½ tsp garam masala
¾ tsp salt or to taste, ½ tsp amchoor (dried mango powder)
½ cup grated paneer (75 gm)
¼ cup chopped green coriander

CRUSH TOGETHER
½ tsp jeera, seeds of 2 moti illaichi, 3-4 saboot kali mirch, 2-3 laung

1. Crush jeera, seeds of moti illaichi, kali mirch and laung together.
2. Clean, wash dal. Pressure cook dal with the above crushed spices, ½ tsp salt and 2 cups water. After the first whistle, keep the cooker on slow fire for 15 minutes. Remove from fire and keep aside.
3. After the pressure drops down, mash the hot dal with a karchhi or a potato masher. If there is any water, mash the dal on fire and dry the dal as well while you are mashing it. Remove from fire.
4. Discard stem of spinach and chop leaves very finely. Wash in several changes of water. Leave the chopped spinach in the strainer for 15 minutes so that the water drains out.
5. Heat 3 tbsp oil in a kadhai. Squeeze and add spinach. Stir for 8-10 minutes till spinach is absolutely dry and well fried.
6. Add paneer and coriander. Cook for 1 minute. Remove from fire and keep aside.
7. Mix dal with - fresh bread crumbs, cornflour, spinach-paneer mixture, green chillies, salt and masalas. Make small balls. Flatten slightly.
8. Cook them on a tawa with just 2-3 tbsp oil till brown on both sides. When done shift them on the sides of the tawa so that they turn crisp and the oil drains out while more kebabs can be added to the hot oil in the centre of the tawa. Remove the kebabs on paper napkins.
9. Serve hot with hari chutney.

Note: If the kebabs break on frying, add 1-2 tbsp of maida to the mixture.

SNACKS

Dakshini Paneer Toasties

A low calorie snack with the South Indian touch.

Picture on page 31   *Serves 4*

75 gm paneer - crumbled (¾ cup)
2 tbsp suji (semolina)
½ tsp salt, or to taste
¼ tsp pepper, or to taste
½ onion - very finely chopped
½ tomato - cut into half, deseeded and chopped finely
2 tbsp curry leaves
3 bread slices - toasted
¼ - ½ tsp rai (small brown mustard seeds)
3 tsp oil to shallow fry

1. Mix the suji, salt and pepper with the paneer using your fingers.
2. Add the onion, tomato and curry leaves.
3. Spread this paneer mixture carefully on the toasted bread slices, keeping the edges neat.
4. Sprinkle some rai over the paneer mixture, pressing down carefully with your finger tips.
5. Heat 1 tsp oil in a non stick frying pan. Add a slice of bread with the topping side down.
6. Cook until it turns golden brown and crisp. Add a little more oil for the next slice if required.
7. Cut into 8 pieces and serve hot.

Note: This recipe will work best using a minimum quantity of oil for frying.

Mushroom Walnut Crackers

Serves 6-8

14-16 cream crackers (salted square biscuits)
1 tbsp butter
100 gm mushrooms - chopped finely
1 onion - chopped
1 tbsp chopped coriander
4 tbsp grated cheese or 2 tbsp cheese spread
1 tbsp walnuts - crushed with a rolling pin (belan)
salt to taste
½ tsp freshly ground pepper
very thin 1" long strips of red or green capsicum

SAUCE
1½ tbsp butter
1½ tbsp maida
1 cup milk

1. Heat 1 tbsp butter in a pan. Add the onion. Saute on medium heat for 1 minute.
2. Add the mushrooms. Saute for 1 minute till water evaporates. Add coriander. Mix. Remove from heat. Keep aside.
3. Heat 1½ tbsp butter in a clean kadhai and add the maida. Cook till slightly brown. Remove from heat.
4. Add the milk gradually, stirring continuously. Return to heat and cook till sauce thickens. Remove from heat.
5. Add mushroom- onion mixture, cheese, walnuts, salt and pepper.
6. At serving time, spread 1-2 tbsp mixture on the cream cracker.
7. Garnish with a thin capsicum strip. Serve.

Mango Chutney Submarine

Picture on facing page   *Serves 4-5*

1 long garlic bread - cut lengthwise to get 2 thin, long pieces
1 tbsp butter - softened
2 tbsp sweet mango chutney (fun food)

TOPPING
1 kheera (cucumber) - cut into round slices without peeling
2 firm tomatoes - cut into round slices
250 gm paneer - cut into ¼" thick, 1½" squares or rounds
few poodina (mint) leaves to garnish - dipped in chilled water
1 tbsp oil

SPRINKLE ON PANEER
¼ tsp haldi, ½ tsp chilli powder, ½ tsp salt, 1 tsp chaat masala powder

1. Spread butter on the cut surface of both the pieces of garlic bread.
2. Place the garlic breads in the oven at 200°C on a wire rack for 10-12 minutes till crisp and light brown on the cut surface. Keep aside.
3. Cut paneer into ¼" thick, big round or square pieces. Use a kulfi mould cover to cut rounds of paneer.
4. Sprinkle the paneer on both sides with some chilli powder, salt, haldi and chaat masala.
5. At serving time, heat 1 tbsp oil in a non stick pan. Saute paneer pieces on both sides in oil till slightly toasted to a nice yellowish-brown colour. Keep aside.
6. To assemble the submarine, apply 1 tbsp mango chutney on each garlic bread.
7. Sprinkle some chaat masala on the kheera and tomato pieces. Sprinkle some chaat masala on the paneer also.
8. Place a piece of paneer (if using square pieces, place them at an angle, pointed side in the centre), then kheera, then tomato and keep repeating all three in the same sequence so as to cover the loaf. Keep paneer, kheera and tomato, slightly overlapping. Insert fresh mint leaves in between the paneer and vegetables, so that they show. Serve.

Note: Mango chutney is available in bottles in stores.

Dakshini Paneer Toasties : Recipe on page 28, Mango Chutney Submarine ➢

Mozzarella Skewers

Stacks of flavour for a starter - slices of oven-toasted bread, mozzarella slices, tomatoes and basil or mint.

Serves 6

3 slices bread
2-3 tbsp olive oil, or any cooking oil
100 gm mozzarella cheese - cut into ¼" thick, 1" squares
2 tomatoes - each cut into 8 pieces and pulp removed
a few fresh basil or mint leaves - dipped in cold water and refrigerated
a few toothpicks
salt to taste
2 tbsp chopped fresh parsley

TO SPRINKLE (MIX TOGETHER), OPTIONAL
2 tbsp vinegar, preferably balsamic vinegar
½ tsp freshly ground pepper or oregano

1. Preheat the oven to 220°C/425°F.
2. Trim the crusts from the bread. Brush the slice with olive oil on both sides. Cut each slice into four equal squares, about the size of the cheese. Arrange on a baking tray and bake for 3-5 minutes until the squares are pale golden.
3. Remove bread squares from the oven and place them on a board.
4. Make 12 stacks - each starting with square of bread, then a slice of mozzarella, a leaf, tomato and again a basil leaf. Sprinkle with salt and pepper.
5. Push a wooden toothpick through each stack and place on a greased baking tray.
6. Drizzle with the remaining oil and bake for 5 minutes at 220°C or until the cheese just begins to melt.
7. Garnish with fresh basil leaves and sprinkle salt and chopped parsley.
8. Spoon a few drops of vinegar mixed with pepper if you like. Serve.

Paneer Kolhapuri

Serves 4

200 gms paneer - cut into 8 big pieces

GRIND TOGETHER TO A PASTE
½" piece ginger
2-3 flakes garlic
2 saboot kali mirch (peppercorns)
2 laung (cloves)
seeds of 2 chhoti illaichi (green cardamoms)
1 tsp jeera (cumin seeds)
2 tsp saboot dhania (coriander seeds)
¾" stick dalchini (cinnamon)
¾ tsp saunf (fennel)
½ tsp red chilli powder
½ tsp salt

COATING
4 tbsp besan
2 tbsp thick curd
1 tbsp chopped fresh dhania (green coriander)
2 tsp kasoori methi (dry fenugreek leaves)
¼ tsp salt, ¼ tsp red chilli powder
¼ tsp ajwain (carom seeds)

1. Grind together ginger, garlic along with all the other ingredients to a fine paste. Use a little water if required.
2. Mix the ground paste with the paneer and cover with a cling film. Keep aside in the refrigerator till the time of serving.
3. At the time of serving, heat oil in a kadhai.
4. Sprinkle the coating ingredients on the paneer and mix well to coat. Add more besan if the paste does not stick to the paneer nicely.
5. Deep fry 2-3 pieces at a time till golden colour.
6. Serve hot with mint chutney, onion rings and lemon wedges.

Baby Chilli Potatoes

Serves 12

250 gm (24) baby potatoes - boiled
1 large capsicum - cut into ½" pieces
¼ cup maida mixed with ½ tsp salt & ¼ cup water to a thick coating batter
3-4 flakes garlic - crushed
1 tbsp vinegar
½ tbsp chilli sauce
1½ tbsp soya sauce
2½ tbsp tomato ketchup
¼ tsp salt and ¼ tsp pepper, or to taste
2 tbsp oil

1. Dip the potatoes in maida batter and deep fry till golden. Keep aside.
2. Heat 2 tbsp oil. Reduce heat. Add garlic. Let it turn light brown.
3. Remove from fire. Add vinegar, soya sauce, tomato sauce and chilli sauce, salt and pepper. Return to fire and cook the sauces on low heat for ½ minute.
4. Add capsicum. Stir for 1-2 minutes.
5. Add fried potatoes and mix well. Remove from fire.
6. Thread a capsicum and then a potato on each tooth pick. Serve.

Corn Kebabs

Crisp and crunchy!

Serves 4

2 tender, large fresh bhuttas - grated (1 cup) or 1 cup tinned or frozen corn, blended coarsely in a grinder, let some kernels remain whole
2 slices bread
1" piece ginger - grated, 1 green chilli - chopped finely
2 tbsp coriander or mint - chopped finely, a few tbsp milk to bind, optional
½ tsp garam masala, ½ tsp amchoor, salt to taste, 2-3 tbsp oil for frying
hari chutney and tomato ketchup to garnish

1. Break the bread slices roughly and grind in a mixer for a few seconds to get fresh bread crumbs. Add bread crumbs to the grated corn.
2. Add chopped coriander or mint, ginger, green chillies, garam masala, amchoor and salt. Mix well. If the mixture feels too dry, add 3-4 tbsp milk to bind the mixture. Shape the mixture into small, round, flattened kebabs.
3. Heat a non stick pan with a little oil. Shallow fry on both sides till golden.
4. Serve dotted with a blob of hari chutney and a dot of tomato ketchup on the hari chutney.

Sun Rise Surprise

Makes 10-12

5-6 slices bread
1 small cucumber - cut into paper-thin slices without peeling - dipped for 30 minutes in ½ cup vinegar to which 1 tsp sugar and 1 tsp salt has been mixed
1 orange, a few fresh or tinned cherries
cheese spread - enough to spread
some bhuna jeera or crushed black pepper
some chaat masala

1. Toast bread slices till crisp. Cut each slice into fancy shapes with a biscuit cutter or cut sides and then into 2 rectangles.
2. Spread cheese spread generously. Sprinkle some bhuna jeera or pepper.
3. Place a pickled cucumber slice. Cut an orange segment into half (keeping the bottom intact) to open it. Cut into half and place it on the side of kheera and top with a cherry.
4. Sprinkle some chaat masala and serve.

Cheese & Spinach Crispies

Serves 6-8

4 slices brown bread
1½ tbsp butter
2-3 flakes garlic - crushed (½ tsp)
100 gm (25-30) leaves of paalak (spinach) - washed & shredded
1½ cups grated paneer (150 gm)
5 tbsp grated mozzarella cheese
1 tbsp chopped coriander
¼ tsp salt and pepper, or taste
½ tsp red chilli flakes

1. Wash and shred spinach leaves into thin ribbons.
2. Heat butter in a kadhai. Add garlic and stir. Squeeze and add spinach and cook till all the moisture of the spinach evaporates. Remove from heat.
3. Mix together - grated paneer, coriander and 4 tbsp grated mozzarella cheese, leaving behind 1 tbsp for the topping.
4. Add cooked spinach to the paneer and mix well. Add salt and pepper.
5. Toast the slices and spread the mixture on the toasts. Sprinkle some mozzarella cheese. Sprinkle some red chilli flakes too.
6. Heat in an oven at 210°C for 2-3 minutes. Cut each slice into 4-8 triangles. Serve hot.

Classic Pizzatini

Serve tiny pizzas with different toppings.

Serves 6

12 readymade cocktail pizza bases
50 gms mozzarella or pizza cheese - grated

TOMATO SPREAD
1 tbsp oil
4-5 flakes of garlic - crushed to a paste (1 tsp)
1/3 cup ready made tomato puree, 1 tbsp tomato sauce
½ tsp oregano (dried), ¼ tsp salt and 2 pinches pepper, or to taste

ADD ONS
1 tbsp tinned sweet corn kernels or thinly sliced baby corns
1 mushroom - cut into paper-thin slices
8-10 spinach leaves, 1 tbsp boiled peas
¼ of a green capsicum - finely chopped (1 tbsp diced)
salt and freshly ground peppercorns and oregano, to taste

1. To prepare the tomato spread, heat 1 tbsp oil. Reduce heat. Add garlic. Stir. Add tomato puree and tomato sauce, salt and pepper. Simmer for 3-4 minutes on low heat. Add oregano. Cook till thick.

2. Boil 2 cups water with ½ tsp salt. Add spinach. Boil. Remove from fire after 1 minute. Strain and chop. Mix boiled peas with spinach.

3. Spread tomato spread on the pizza bases, leaving the edges clean. Sprinkle some cheese on the tomato spread, reserving some for top.

4. Put corn on 4 bases, mushrooms on the other 4 and blanched spinach and peas on the last 4 bases. Spread capsicum on the mushroom and corn pizzatinis. Sprinkle some salt and pepper. Sprinkle the remaining cheese on all of them. Sprinkle some oregano too on the cheese.

5. Place the pizzas on the wire rack of a hot oven (200°C). Grill for about 8-10 minutes till the base gets crisp and the cheese melts. To get a crisp pizza, oil the bottom of the base a little before grilling.

6. Serve them all together on a platter without cutting, along with some red chilli flakes and mustard sauce.

Note: To make mustard sauce, mix a little cream with some ready-made English mustard paste to get the saucy consistency. To make chilli flakes, coarsely dry-grind the whole red chillies in a small spice grinder.

Peanut Broccoli Balls

Serves 8

200 gm broccoli (1 small head) - chopped finely along with tender stalks (1½ cups)
1 onion - chopped finely
¼ cup roasted peanuts - coarsely crushed on a chakla-belan (rolling board & pin)
1 tbsp butter

SAUCE
3 tbsp melted butter
4 tbsp maida (plain flour)
1 cup milk
¼ tsp each salt & pepper, or to taste

COATING
½ cup maida mixed with ½ cup water
1 cup dry bread crumbs
oil for frying

1. Break broccoli into florets and wash well. Chop the broccoli florets and the tender stems very finely.
2. Heat butter in a pan. Add chopped onion. Stir and add the chopped broccoli. Add 2 pinches of salt. Cook on medium heat for about 2-3 minutes on low heat, till slightly tender. Remove from heat.
3. Add peanuts to broccoli. Keep aside.
4. To prepare the sauce, heat butter in a clean pan. Add maida and cook till maida turns slightly brown.
5. Remove from heat and add milk, stirring continuously. Return to heat. Cook till the sauce thickens and starts leaving the sides of the pan.
6. Add salt, pepper and cooked broccoli. Cook further for 1-2 minutes on low heat. Remove from heat. Cool well.
7. Slightly wet your hands and make balls of the cold broccoli mixture. If the mixture is even slightly warm, it becomes difficult to make balls. Keep in the refrigerator till serving time.
8. Prepare the coating mixture by mixing maida and water. Add a pinch of salt and pepper to it.
9. Heat oil in a kadhai. Dip balls in the coating mixture and roll in bread crumbs. Fry till golden brown. Drain on absorbent paper. Serve hot.

Hariyaali Idlis

Delicious green-paalak idlis. They taste good even without sambhar & chutney.

Serves 8

1 packet (200 gm) ready-made idli mix
1½ cups chopped spinach, 2-3 green chillies - deseeded & chopped
a few cashewnuts or blanched almonds - split into two halves, optional

TOPPING
2 cups fresh curd - beat well till smooth
½ tsp salt

TEMPERING (TADKA)
2 tbsp oil
1 tsp rai (small brown mustard seeds)
½ tsp jeera (cumin seeds)
2 green chillies - chopped
1 small tomato - chopped finely
20-30 curry leaves

1. Mix the idli mix according to the instructions on the packet.
2. Grind the chopped spinach and green chillies in a mixer and grind to a smooth puree or a paste with 1-2 tbsp water.
3. Add the spinach paste to the idli mixture. Add ¼ tsp salt to it.
4. Grease a mini idli mould. Put a little batter in each cup and top with a split cashewnut or almond on each idli. Steam for 14-15 minutes on medium flame till a knife inserted in the idli comes out clean. If a mini mould is not available, make small flat idlis by putting a little less batter in the normal idli mould.
5. Place the steamed idlis in a large bowl.
6. Beat the curd with salt till smooth. Pour the curd over the idlis in the bowl. Mix gently. Keep aside for 10-15 minutes.
7. Transfer the idlis to a flat serving platter or a shallow dish. Keep aside till serving time.
8. At the time of serving, heat 2 tbsp oil. Add rai and jeera. When they stop spluttering, add green chillies, tomato and curry leaves. Stir to mix all ingredients and immediately pour over the idlis covered with curd. Serve.

Pao Bhaji

Picture on facing page   *Serves 6*

250 gms (3 big) boiled potatoes - mashed roughly
½ cup shelled peas
2 small carrots - chopped finely
10-12 french beans - chopped finely
200-250 gms (½ of a small flower) cabbage - chopped finely
200-250 gms cauliflower (½ of a small flower) - chopped finely
400 gms (5 big) tomatoes - chopped finely
200 gms (2 big) onions - chopped finely
2-4 green chillies - chopped finely
1 tbsp ginger-garlic paste
2 tbsp pao-bhaji masala
50 gms butter
4-5 tbsp oil
1½ tsp salt, or to taste
1 tbsp chopped coriander

1. Chop all vegetables finely.
2. Pressure cook peas, carrots, french beans, cauliflower and cabbage with ½ cup water to give one whistle. Keep on low flame for 5 minutes.
3. Heat oil. Add onions and green chillies. Cook till onions turn golden.
4. Add tomatoes and bhuno for 5-7 minutes. Mash them well.
5. Add ginger-garlic paste and cook for 2-3 minutes on low flame.
6. Add pao-bhaji masala and salt.
7. Add pressure cooked vegetables and potatoes. Cook for a few minutes, mashing them continuously.
8. Add butter and chopped coriander. Serve hot, with buns cut into halves and tossed in butter on a tawa.

Minty Mushroom Balls

Serves 8-10

4 boiled potatoes - mashed or grated
2 tbsp grated cheese, a pinch of baking powder
2 slices of bread - ground in a mixer to get fresh crumbs
¼ cup chopped mint (poodina)
½ tsp garam masala, ½ tsp red chilli powder, ¼ tsp amchoor
salt to taste
oil for frying
dry bread crumbs to coat

FILLING
1 tbsp butter
150 gms mushrooms - chopped (1½ cups)
1 large onion - chopped (½ cup)
salt and pepper to taste
¼ cup finely chopped mint leaves (poodina)
1 tsp lemon juice

1. Boil potatoes. Mash well while still hot or grate them if they have turned cold.
2. To the mashed potatoes, add cheese, baking powder, bread, mint, garam masala, red chilli powder, amchoor and salt to taste. Mix well. Keep aside.
3. To prepare the filling, heat butter in a pan. Add onions and cook till soft. Add mushrooms. Saute for 3-4 minutes and let them turn dry.
4. Add mint, lemon juice, salt and pepper to taste. Mix well. Remove from heat.
5. Divide the potato mixture into 8 balls. Flatten each potato ball to a diameter of about 3".
6. Place 1 tbsp of mushroom and mint filling on it. Press. Cover the filling by lifting the sides of the potato. Shape into a ball.
7. Roll over bread crumbs to coat.
8. Heat oil and fry till golden brown. Serve with tomato ketchup or hari chutney.

Cheese Pockets

Crisp cheesy pockets - Great combination with any soup.

Serves 4

1 thick pizza base
1/3 cup mozzarella cheese
1/3 cup processed cheese (cheese cubes)
1 tsp oregano (dried)
2 tbsp finely chopped onion
2 tbsp finely chopped capsicum or coriander
2 tbsp butter or olive oil
red chilli flakes or a few freshly crushed peppercorns

1. Heat oven to 200°C.
2. Cut the pizza base into half and then each half into half again to get 4 triangles. Split each triangle from the pointed end almost till the edge, leaving the edges intact, to get a pocket.
3. Mix both the cheese, onion, capsicum or coriander and oregano. Add a pinch of salt.
4. Fill the pockets with cheese mixture, keeping aside some for the top.
5. Place on a baking tray. Brush the triangles generously with butter or olive oil.
6. Sprinkle left over cheese mixture. Pour some melted butter or oil on the cheese.
7. Sprinkle chilli flakes or crushed peppercorns.
8. Grill for 5-6 minutes until slightly brown and crisp.
9. Cut each piece into 3 pieces with a pizza cutter. Serve hot.

Naaza

Naan spread with an Indian tomato spread flavoured with kasoori methi, topped with paneer tikkas and mozzarella cheese.

Picture on back cover   *Serves 4*

2 ready made nans
100-150 gms pizza cheese

TOMATO SPREAD
1-2 tbsp oil
4 flakes garlic - crushed
2 small tomatoes - pureed in a mixer
¼ tsp salt, ¼ tsp garam masala, ¼ tsp red chilli powder
2 tbsp tomato sauce, 2 tsp kasoori methi

TOPPING
100 gms paneer - cut into ½" squares, 2 tsp kasoori methi
½ green and ½ yellow capsicum - cut into ½" squares, or 1 green one
1 tomato - cut into 4 pieces and deseeded and cut into ½" pieces
1½ tbsp oil, ½ onion - cut into ½" squares
¼ tsp each - salt, red chilli, haldi and garam masala, or to taste
1 tbsp tomato puree, ½ tsp ginger-garlic paste

YOGURT CHUTNEY (MIX TOGETHER)
2 tbsp hari chutney, 3 tbsp curd - whipped till smooth
a pinch of kala namak and bhuna jeera

1. To prepare the tomato spread, heat oil. Add garlic and all other ingredients. Cook till thick.
2. For the topping, heat 1½ tbsp oil. Add onion. Saute till golden. Reduce heat. Add salt, red chilli, haldi and garam masala. Mix. Add tomato puree and ginger-garlic paste. Add capsicums and tomato. Mix.
3. Add paneer and kasoori methi. Mix well and remove from fire.
4. Brush the naan with 1 tsp oil. Spread some tomato spread.
5. Sprinkle some pizza cheese.
6. Spread paneer topping. Sprinkle some cheese again.
7. Grill for about 15 minutes at 200°C till the paneer gets grilled and the edges of the nan turn brown. Do not over grill, it turns hard! Cut into pieces and serve hot with yogurt chutney.

INDIAN CURRIES

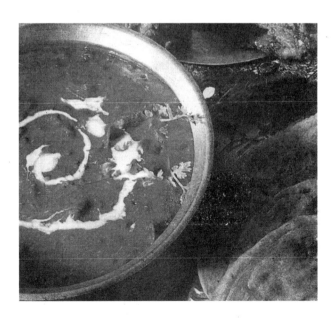

Vegetable Korma

Curd, coconut and cashews form the base of a good korma. A little cream (¼ cup) can be added at the time of serving.

Serves 4

½ cup shelled peas
2 small carrots - cut into round slices
6 french beans - cut into ½" diagonal pieces
6-8 small florets (1" pieces) of cauliflower - fried till golden and cooked
1-2 small slices of tinned pineapple - cut into 1" pieces, optional (see note)
4 tbsp oil
2 onions - chopped finely
¼ tsp haldi (turmeric) powder
½ tsp garam masala
2 tsp salt

GRIND TOGETHER (CASHEW-CURD PASTE)
3 tbsp cashews - soaked in warm water for 10 minutes and drained
3/4 cup curd
2 tbsp grated coconut (fresh or desiccated)
½" piece ginger
3-4 flakes garlic
2 tsp dhania saboot (coriander seeds)
seeds of 2-3 chhoti illaichi (green cardamom)

1. Soak cashews. Drain. Grind them with coconut, ginger, garlic, saboot dhania and chhoti illaichi together to a paste alongwith curd.
2. Heat oil. Add onions. Cook till onions turn golden brown.
3. Add haldi. Stir to mix well.
4. Add the cashew-curd paste. Cook on low heat for 3-4 minutes.
5. Add salt and garam masala. Stir for a few seconds.
6. Add french beans, peas and carrots. Stir for 2 minutes.
7. Add 1½ cup water or enough to get a thick gravy. Boil. Simmer covered for 8-10 minutes till the vegetables get done.
8. Add cauliflower and pineapple. Boil for 1 minute.
9. Serve sprinkled with chopped coriander.

Note: The left over pineapple can be stored in a steel or plastic box in the freezer compartment of the refrigerator without getting spoilt.

Shahi Baby Corns

Baby corns in a red shahi gravy. If baby corns are not available, regular corn on the cob can be used instead.

Serves 8

200 gm baby corns or 2 small tender bhutte (corn on the cobs)
½-1 cup milk, approx.
2 tbsp cashews - soaked for 10 minutes and ground to a paste with ¼ cup water

MASALA
2 small onions, 4 tomatoes, 1" piece ginger, 1 green chilli - grind to a paste
4 tbsp oil, ½ tsp shah jeera
1 tsp dhania (coriander) powder, ½ tsp amchoor, 1½ tsp salt
½ tsp red chilli powder, 1 tsp garam masala
1 tsp tandoori masala
2-3 chhoti illaichi (green cardamom) - seeds crushed
50 -100 gms paneer - grated (½-1 cup), 3 tbsp chopped coriander

BAGHAR OR TEMPERING
1 tbsp oil, ½ tsp shah jeera (black cumin), 1 tsp finely chopped ginger
5-6 almonds (badaam) - cut into thin long pieces, ¼ tsp red chilli powder

1. Choose small baby corns or thin tender bhuttas. Keep baby corns whole or cut each bhutta into 4 small pieces. If thick, slit each piece into two.
2. Put all the pieces of baby corns and ½ cup milk in a pan. Give one boil and keep on low heat for 2 minutes. If using bhuttas, use a pressure cooker to cook the them. Pressure cook bhutta pieces with 1 cup milk to give one whistle. Then keep on low flame for 5 minutes. Remove from fire.
3. Blend onions, tomatoes, green chilli and ginger to a paste in a grinder.
4. Heat oil. Add shah jeera. After a minute, add onion-tomato paste and cook till dry and oil separates. Reduce flame. Add red chilli powder, dhania, amchoor, salt and garam masala. Cook for 1 minute.
5. Add cashew paste. Stir to mix well.
6. Keeping the flame low, add the left over milk from the boiled bhuttas, stirring continuously. Stir for 2-3 minutes.
7. Add corn and simmer on low flame for 3 minutes. Add enough (2-3 cups approx.) water to get a thin gravy. Boil. Simmer for 5-7 minutes till slightly thick. Add tandoori masala, chhoti illaichi, paneer and coriander.
8. Transfer to a serving dish. Heat oil. Add jeera and ginger. After a few seconds, add almonds and stir. Add red chilli powder, remove from fire and pour the oil on the gravy. Serve.

Kandhari Khumb

Picture on cover   *Serves 6-8*

300 gm mushrooms
juice of ½ lemon, 1 tsp salt
1 tbsp butter, ¼ tsp pepper
½ cup red kandhari anaar ke dane (fresh pomegranate)

GRAVY
3 onions
1½" piece ginger
2 dry red chillies
4-5 chhoti illaichi (green cardamoms)
4 tbsp kaju (cashewnuts) - powdered
4 tbsp oil
½ tsp garam masala, ¾ tsp red chilli powder, 1½ tsp salt, or to taste
1 cup milk mixed with 2 cups water
2 tbsp cream, optional

1. Wash mushrooms and trim the stalks.
2. Boil 4 cups water with 1 tsp salt and juice of ½ lemon. Add the trimmed mushrooms. Boil for 2 minutes. Drain and refresh with cold water. Wipe to dry well.
3. Heat 1 tbsp butter and saute mushrooms on high heat till dry. Sprinkle pepper and mix. Remove from fire.
4. To prepare the gravy, grind onions, ginger and dry red chillies to a fine paste.
5. Heat 4 tbsp oil in a heavy bottomed kadhai and add chhoti illaichi. Wait for ½ minute.
6. Add onion paste. Cook on low flame for about 10-15 minutes till onions turn light brown and oil separates.
7. Add masalas - garam masala, red chilli powder and salt.
8. Add kaju powder. Cook for ½ minute.
9. Add milk mixed with water, to make a gravy. Boil. Simmer on low flame for 5 minutes.
10. Add anaar ke dane, keeping aside a little for garnishing.
11. To serve, boil gravy. Add mushrooms. Keep on low heat for ½ a minute. Serve immediately, sprinkled with cream and dotted with anaar.

Water Melon Curry

An unusual & spicy, thin reddish curry. Enjoy it with Southern curd rice or plain boiled rice!

Serves 4   Picture on page 117

4 cups of tarbooz (water melon) - cut into 1" pieces along with a little white portion also, and deseeded
4-5 flakes garlic - crushed
2 tbsp oil
½ tsp jeera (cumin seeds)
a pinch of hing (asafoetida)
1 tbsp ginger - cut into thin match sticks (juliennes)
½ tsp dhania (coriander) powder
½ - ¾ tsp chilli powder
a pinch of haldi powder
½ tsp salt, or to taste
2 tsp lemon juice

GARNISH
sliced green chillies & chopped green coriander

1. Puree 1½ cups of water melon cubes (the upper soft pieces) with 4-5 flakes of garlic to get 1 cup of water melon puree. Leave the remaining firm, lower pieces (with the white portion) as it is. Keep aside.
2. Heat oil in a kadhai or a pan. Add hing and jeera. Let jeera turn·golden.
3. Add garlic and shredded ginger and stir for ½ minute.
4. Add the remaining water melon pieces or cubes and stir to mix.
5. Sprinkle coriander powder, red chilli powder and haldi. Stir for ½ minute.
6. Add the water melon puree, salt and lemon juice. Simmer for 2-3 minutes till you get a thin curry. Remove from fire.
7. Garnish with green chillies and green coriander. Serve hot with boiled rice.

Manzil-e-Paneer

A quick attractive way of serving paneer.

Picture on facing page   *Serves 8*

700-800 gm paneer - cut into a long, thick slab (7" long and 2" thick, approx.)
2-3 tbsp grated cheese

FILLING (MIX TOGETHER)
¼ cup grated carrot (½ carrot), ½ cup grated cabbage, 2 tbsp grated cheese
¼ tsp salt and ¼ tsp freshly ground pepper, or to taste

TOMATO SAUCE
5 tomatoes - chopped roughly & boiled with ½ cup water
6 tbsp ready made tomato puree, 2 tbsp oil, 1 tsp crushed garlic (6-8 flakes)
½ tsp black pepper, ½ tsp salt and ¼ tsp pepper, or to taste, 3 tbsp cream

1. To prepare the sauce, boil chopped tomatoes in ½ cup water. Keep on low heat for 4-5 minutes till soft. Remove from fire. Mash and strain. Discard the skin. Keep fresh tomato puree aside.
2. Heat oil. Reduce heat. Add garlic and stir till it just starts to change colour. Do not make it brown.
3. Add 6 tbsp ready made tomato puree. Cook till oil separates, for about 2-3 minutes on medium flame.
4. Add the prepared fresh tomato puree and give one boil. Simmer on low heat for 5-6 minutes. Remove from fire. Cool to room temperature.
5. Mix in cream. Add salt & pepper to taste and keep the sauce aside.
6. Cut paneer into 3 equal pieces lengthwise. Sprinkle salt and pepper on both sides of each slice of paneer.
7. In a shallow rectangular serving dish, put ¼ of the prepared sauce.
8. Place a paneer slab on the sauce.
9. Spread ½ of the carrot-cabbage filling on it.
10. Press another piece of paneer on it.
11. Again put the filling on it. Cover with the last piece of paneer. Press.
12. Pour the sauce all over the paneer to cover the top and the sides completely. Grate cheese on top. Sprinkle some pepper.
13. If using a microwave, cover loosely with a cling film and micro high for 2 minutes. If using an ordinary oven, cover loosely with aluminium foil and heat for 8-10 minutes in a moderately hot oven at 180°C till hot.

Lychee Pearls : Recipe on page 123, Manzil-e-Paneer ➤

Baingan Aur Mirch Ka Saalan

Serves 4

4-5 achaari hari mirch (large, thick green chillies)
6 small brinjals - cut into 4 pieces lengthwise and sprinkled with salt
a lemon sized ball of imli (tamarind)
5 tbsp oil
½ tsp sarson (mustard seeds), ½ tsp kalonji (onion seeds)
3 onions - finely chopped
2 tbsp fresh cream

GRIND TOGETHER TO A SMOOTH PASTE
2 tbsp til (sesame seeds)
2 tbsp peanuts
1 tsp desiccated coconut (coconut powder), optional
6 flakes garlic
1½" piece of ginger
2 tsp coriander powder
¼ tsp haldi (turmeric) powder
1 tsp jeera
1 tsp salt
1 tsp fresh lemon juice

1. Wash the tamarind and put in a bowl with 1½ cups hot water. Mash and leave it to soak for 10 minutes.
2. Grind the sesame seeds, peanuts, coconut, ginger, garlic, coriander, turmeric, jeera, salt and lemon juice to a paste with a little water. Keep aside.
3. Pat dry the brinjals sprinkled with salt on a clean kitchen towel.
4. Heat 5-6 tbsp oil in pan. Reduce heat and fry the green chillies for 1½ minutes. Remove the chillies from the oil and keep aside. In the same oil, add the brinjals. Fry turning sides on medium heat till they change colour and turn brownish. Check with a knife and remove from oil when they turn soft.
5. Heat 2 tbsp oil and add kalonji and sarson. Wait for ½ minute till they crackle, add onions and curry leaves. Fry till onions turn golden brown.
6. Add the freshly ground paste and fry for 1-2 minutes.
7. Add 2 cups water in the pan and stir and then pour strained tamarind juice into the pan. Boil. Simmer for 7-8 minutes on low heat.
8. Add the green chillies and brinjals. Cook for 5 minutes on low heat.
9. Reduce heat. Add cream and remove from fire. Serve with rice or chappati.

Malai Khumb Matar

Serves 4-5   *Picture on page 87*

200 gms mushrooms - preferably small in size
1 cup shelled, boiled or frozen peas
4 tbsp kasoori methi (dry fenugreek leaves)
1 tsp ginger-garlic paste
1 tbsp butter, 3 tbsp oil
2 onions - ground to a paste
¼ cup malai (milk topping) - mix with ¼ cup milk and blend in a mixer for a few
seconds till smooth or ½ cup thin fresh cream
1 tsp salt to taste
½ tsp red chilli powder, ½ tsp garam masala
a pinch of amchoor
½ cup milk (approx.)

GRIND TOGETHER
½ stick dalchini (cinnamon)
seeds of 2-3 chhoti illaichi (green cardamom)
3-4 laung (cloves)
4-5 saboot kali mirch (peppercorns)
2 tbsp cashewnuts

1. Trim the stem of each mushroom. Leave them whole if small or cut them into 2 pieces, if big. Heat 1 tbsp butter in a kadhai and add the mushrooms. Stir fry on high flame till dry and golden. Add 1 tsp ginger-garlic paste, ½ tsp salt and a pinch of white or black pepper. Stir for 1 more minute and remove from fire. Keep cooked mushrooms aside.
2. Grind together dalchini, seeds of chhoti illaichi, laung, kali mirch and cashew to a powder in a small mixer grinder.
3. Heat 3 tbsp oil. Add onion paste and cook on low heat till oil separates. Do not let the onions turn brown.
4. Add the freshly ground masala-cashew powder. Cook for a few seconds.
5. Add the kasoori methi and malai, cook on low heat for 2-3 minutes till malai dries up.
6. Add salt, red chilli powder, garam masala and amchoor. Stir for 1 minute.
7. Add the boiled peas and mushrooms.
8. Add ½ cup milk to get a thick gravy. Add ½ cup water if the gravy appears too thick. Boil for 2-3 minutes. Serve.

Paneer Pasanda

Stuffed paneer in a light yogurt based gravy

Serves 6-8

400 gm paneer - cut into slices of ¼" thickness
1 tsp shah jeera (black cumin)
¼ tsp red chilli powder, 1 tsp salt
1½ cups milk, approx.
green coriander - to garnish

FILLING
4 tbsp grated mozzarella cheese
1 tsp very finely chopped ginger
1 green chilli - deseeded & chopped very finely
a pinch of haldi, a pinch of salt, or to taste, a pinch of red chilli powder
2 tsp kishmish - chopped finely

ONION-TOMATO PASTE (GRIND TOGETHER)
2 onions - roughly sliced
2 tomatoes - roughly sliced
2 green chillies - chopped
2" piece ginger - chopped
1 cup curd

1. Mix all ingredients of the filling. Spread on a piece of paneer. Place the other piece of paneer on it. Press. Cut the sides to make neat squares. Saute in 2 tbsp oil on a tawa or nonstick pan on medium heat using 2 flat spoons, till golden on both sides. After it cools, cut each piece into 2 triangles. Keep aside.

2. Grind onion, tomato, green chillies, ginger and curd in a mixer and grind to a smooth paste.

3. Heat 4 tbsp oil. Add shah jeera. Wait for 1 minute.

4. Add the onion-tomato paste and cook till the water evaporates and the masala thickens. Add the salt and chilli powder. Mix well. Cook till oil separates.

5. Keeping the heat low, add milk and 1½ cups water to get a gravy. Stir continuously on low heat to give a boil. Simmer for 4-5 minutes on low heat. Remove from fire. Keep aside.

6. At serving time, pour most of the gravy at the bottom of a shallow serving dish. Arrange paneer in a single layer over it. Pour the left over gravy on it. Heat in a microwave or oven.

Quick Rajmah Curry

Servings 4-6

1½ cups lal rajmah (red kidney beans) - soaked overnight
1 tbsp channe ki dal (split gram) - soaked overnight
2 tsp salt or to taste
1 onion - chopped finely
6-8 flakes garlic - crushed, 1" piece ginger - chopped finely
4 tbsp oil
3 tomatoes - pureed in a blender
½ cup curd - beat well till smooth
3 tsp dhania powder, ¼ tsp amchoor
½ tsp garam masala, ½ tsp chilli powder (or to taste), a pinch of haldi
2 laung (cloves) - crushed
2 tbsp chopped coriander

1. Pressure cook rajmah, channe ki dal, salt, chopped onion, garlic and ginger together with enough water to give 1 whistle. Keep on low flame for ½ hour. Remove from fire.
2. Heat 4 tbsp oil in a heavy bottomed kadhai. Add tomatoes pureed in a blender. Cook till tomatoes turn dry.
3. Reduce flame and add dhania powder, amchoor, garam masala, red chilli powder and haldi. Cook till oil separates.
4. Add beaten curd and stir continuously on low flame till the masala turns red again and oil separates.
5. Add crushed laung.
6. Strain and add the rajmahs, leaving behind the water. Stir fry on low flame for 5-7 minutes, mashing occasionally.
7. Add the rajmahs to the water in the pressure cooker and pressure cook to give 1 whistle. Keep on low heat for 8-10 minutes. Remove from fire.
8. Garnish with freshly chopped coriander leaves. Serve hot with chappatis or boiled rice.

Dal Makhani

Picture on page 69   *Serves 6*

1 cup urad saboot (whole black beans)
2 tbsp channe ki dal (split gram dal)
2 whole, dry red chillies - soaked in water for 10 minutes
1 tbsp ghee or oil
5 cups of water
1½ tsp salt
1" piece ginger
4 flakes garlic (optional)
4 tomatoes - pureed in a grinder
2-3 tbsp butter
1 tbsp kasoori methi
½ tsp garam masala
2 tsp tomato ketchup
½ cup milk, approx.
½ cup fresh cream
¼ tsp grated jaiphal (nutmeg)

1. Grind ginger, garlic and dry red chillies together to a paste.
2. Clean, wash dals. Pressure cook both dals with 1 tbsp ghee, water, salt and ginger-garlic paste.
3. After the first whistle, keep on low flame for 40 minutes. Remove from fire. Keep aside for the pressure to drop.
4. Add tomatoes pureed in a grinder to the dal.
5. Add butter and kasoori methi.
6. Add garam masala and tomato ketchup. Simmer on slow fire for 8-10 minutes, stirring occasionally. Keep mashing the dal slightly in between.
7. Add some milk if the dal appears too thick. Cook till it reaches the right consistency.
8. Add cream and jaiphal. Remove from fire. Serve hot.

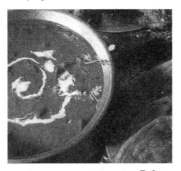

Palak Chaman

Serves 4

500 gms paalak (spinach) - chopped (5 cups)
4 tbsp kasoori methi (dry fenugreek leaves)
1 cup chopped coriander
1 green chilli
1 tsp sugar
2 tbsp besan (gram flour)
1 potato - cut into ½" cubes and deep fried till golden & cooked
½ stick dalchini (cinnamon)
2 chhoti illaichi (green cardamoms)
3-4 laung (cloves)
5 tbsp oil
2 onions - ground to a paste
½ cup cream or milk, approx.
1 tsp salt, or to taste

BAGHAR
1 tbsp desi ghee, 1 tbsp chopped ginger, ½ tsp red chilli powder

1. Boil spinach, kasoori methi, fresh coriander and green chilli in 1 cup water with sugar. Cook on low flame for 4-5 minutes till spinach turns soft. Remove from fire.
2. Strain the spinach and keep the liquid aside. Cool the spinach and blend to a puree.
3. Mix besan with the spinach liquid and keep aside.
4. Fry potatoes till golden brown and cooked. Keep aside.
5. Crush dalchini, laung and seeds of chhoti illaichi to a rough powder. Keep aside.
6. Heat 5 tbsp oil. Add onions and cook on low heat till oil separates and they turn light brown.
7. Add the freshly ground masala. Cook for a few seconds.
8. Add besan dissolved in liquid. Cook for 2 minutes.
9. Add the palak puree. Bhuno for 5-7 minutes till dry and oil separates.
10. Add enough cream or milk, to get the right consistency and colour. Cook on low heat for 2 minutes.
11. Add the fried potatoes.
12. Add salt to taste. Simmer for a few minutes. Transfer to a serving dish.
13. To serve, heat 1 tbsp desi ghee for the baghar. Add ginger. Remove from fire. When ginger turns golden, add red chilli powder to the hot oil. Remove from fire and mix lightly with the spinach. Serve hot.

INDIAN -
DRY & MASALA

Subz Paneer Jalfrezi

Serves 4

150 gm paneer - cut into thin long pieces
8-10 french beans - sliced diagonally into 1" pieces
1 large carrot - cut diagonally into thin slices
½ green capsicum - deseed and cut into thin fingers
½ yellow or red pepper (capsicum) - deseeded & sliced into thin fingers
1 long, firm tomato - cut into 4, pulp removed and cut into thin long pieces
3 tbsp oil
½ tsp jeera (cumin seeds), ¼ tsp sarson (mustard seeds)
¼ tsp kalonji (onion seeds), ¼ tsp methi daana (fenugreek seeds)
15-20 curry leaves

MIX TOGETHER
3 tbsp tomato puree, 1 tbsp tomato ketchup
2 tsp ginger-garlic paste or 2 tsp ginger-garlic - finely chopped
½ tsp red chilli powder, ½ tsp amchoor powder, 1 tsp dhania powder, ¾ tsp salt

1. Mix together - tomato puree, tomato ketchup, ginger, garlic, red chilli powder, dhania powder, amchoor and salt in a bowl. Keep aside.
2. Heat 3 tbsp oil in a kadhai. Add jeera, sarson, kalonji and methi dana. When jeera turns golden, reduce heat and add curry leaves and stir for a few seconds.
3. Add the tomato puree mixed with dry masalas and stir on medium heat for 2 minutes.
4. Add carrot and beans. Stir for 1 minute.
5. Add ¼ cup water. Cover the kadhai. Cook on low heat for about 4-5 minutes, till vegetables are cooked but still remain crunchy.
6. Add the capsicums, paneer and tomato. Stir till well blended. Remove from fire. Serve hot.

Kastoori Gobhi

Fried cauliflower, cooked with capsicum and tomato in masala.

Serves 4

1 medium cauliflower - cut into medium size florets with a little stalk
1 tsp jeera (cumin seeds)
2 onions - chopped
1½ tbsp ginger-garlic paste
2- 4 green chillies - deseeded & chopped
¼ tsp garam masala
¼ tsp red chilli powder, 1 tsp salt or to taste
1 tbsp kasoori methi (dry fenugreek leaves)
½ cup dahi (yoghurt) - beat till smooth
1 tomato - cut into 8 big pieces
1 large capsicum - cut into 1" cubes

1. Break the cauliflower into medium florets, keeping the stalk intact.
2. Heat oil in a kadhai for deep frying. Add all the cauliflower pieces and fry to a light brown colour. Remove from oil and keep aside.
3. Heat 2 tbsp oil. Add jeera. When it turns golden, add chopped onions. Stir till golden.
4. Add the ginger-garlic paste, green chillies, salt, chilli powder, garam masala, kasoori methi and curd. Stir-fry for 2-3 minutes till the curd dries up a little.
5. Add capsicum and tomato cubes. Fry for 1-2 minutes.
6. Add cauliflower and mix well on low heat for 2 minutes till the gobhi get well blended with the masala. Serve hot.

Kurkuri Ajwaini Bhindi

Crisp fried bhindi flavoured with carom seeds.

Serves 2-3

250 gm bhindi (lady fingers)
3 tbsp besan (gram flour), ½ tsp ajwain (carom seeds)
¼ tsp haldi
2 tsp chaat masala
1 tsp ginger paste
juice of ½ lemon (1 tbsp)
½ tsp salt, or to taste
1 tsp chilli powder
oil for frying

1. Wash and pat dry bhindi. Cut the head (the stem end) and slit the bhindi into four lengthwise. Place in a shallow bowl or paraat.
2. Sprinkle ajwain, haldi, chaat masala, ginger paste on the bhindi.
3. Just before serving, add salt, dry besan and lemon juice and mix well to coat the bhindi.
4. Heat oil for deep frying. Add half of the bhindi to hot oil and fry in 2 batches till crisp. Drain on absorbent paper. Serve hot.

Note: Mix all the ingredients to the bhindi at the time of frying as the salt added releases moisture which can make the bhindi soggy.

Subz Bahaar

Serves 4-5

2 small capsicums - cut into 8 pieces (1" cubes)
2 boiled potatoes - cut into 6 pieces (1" cubes)
2 carrots - peeled
6-8 baby corns
10 mushrooms - keep whole
1 tomato - cut into 8 pieces (1" cubes)
juice of 1 lemon
4 tbsp oil
½ tsp jeera
1" piece ginger - chopped
¼ tsp haldi

MASALA POWDER
seeds of 3 chhoti illaichi (green cardamoms)
seeds of 2 moti illaichi (black cardamom)
2-3 laung (cloves)
1" stick dalchini (cinnamon)

1. Boil 3 cups water with 1 tsp salt. Add the whole carrots, baby corns and mushrooms. After the boil returns keep on fire for 2 minutes. (Do not over cook). Remove from fire and let the vegetables be in hot water for 2-3 minutes. Strain and refresh in cold water. Strain and keep aside.
2. Cut carrots into ½" thick, round slices. Cut baby corns into 2 pieces if big. Leave mushrooms whole. Wipe dry all vegetables.
3. Meanwhile, crush all ingredients of the masala powder to a rough powder.
4. Heat oil in a kadhai. Add jeera. Let it turn golden. Add haldi. Add potatoes and bhuno for 4-5 minutes. Keep potatoes spread out so that they turn crisp and do not stir too often.
5. Add ginger. Stir for a minute.
6. Add mushrooms, baby corns and carrots. Stir for 4-5 minutes till the vegetables get cooked and brown. Add 1 tsp salt (or to taste) and 1½ tsp masala powder.
7. Add capsicum and tomatoes together. Add ¼ tsp salt. Stir fry for 2 minutes.
8. Squeeze lemon juice. Serve.

Achaari Baingans

Serves 4

250 gm chhote baingan (brinjals)
3 tbsp oil
½ tsp kalonji, ½ tsp sarson, ¼ tsp methi dana
2-3 red chillies
2 tbsp curry leaves
3 tbsp tamarind pulp (soak a marble size ball of imli in ½ cup warm water and
squeeze to extract pulp)
1 tsp sugar, or to taste

GRIND TO A PASTE
3-4 flakes garlic (1 tsp chopped)
1" piece ginger
1 small onion
2 tsp saunf (fennel)
½ tsp each of garam masala, haldi & red chilli powder
1 tsp dhania powder, 1 tsp amchoor powder, 1½ tsp salt

1. Wash baingans and give two cuts crossing each other, more than half way, almost till the end, keeping the end intact. Keep aside.
2. Grind all ingredients together with 2 tbsp water.
3. Fill the brinjals nicely with the masala, pushing it down with a knife.
4. Heat 3 tbsp oil in a big, heavy bottomed kadhai. Add kalonji, sarson and methi dana.
5. Reduce heat. Add dry red chillies and curry leaves.
6. When methi dana turns golden, add baingans. Stir to mix well. Add the left over masala, if any. Cover and cook, spreading them in the kadhai and stirring occasionally, for 15 minutes or till done. Do not stir frequently, otherwise they might break.
7. Add the sugar and tamarind pulp. Mix. Serve hot.

Kadhai Baby Corns

Serves 4

12-15 baby corns (200 gm)
2 capsicums - cut into fingers
2 dry red chillies
1½ tsp saboot dhania (coriander seeds)
1½ " piece ginger- chopped finely
1" piece ginger - shredded on the grater
10-12 flakes garlic- crushed
1 onion - finely chopped
1 green chilli - chopped
3 tomatoes- chopped
3 tbsp tomato puree
a pinch of methi daana (fenugreek seeds)
¾ tsp salt
5 tbsp oil

1. Boil 4 cups water with 2 tsp salt and 2 tsp lemon juice. Add corn and boil for 2 minutes. Drain.
2. Warm red chillies on a tawa, till slightly crisp and dry.
3. Pound red chillies and saboot dhania to a rough powder (chakla belan can be used.)
4. Heat 2 tbsp oil in a kadhai and add the boiled baby corns. Bhuno for 4-5 minutes. Add the capsicum strips and stir fry for 2 minutes. Remove from kadhai and keep aside.
5. Heat 3 tbsp oil in a kadhai. Reduce flame. Add a pinch of methi daana and garlic. Bhuno for a few seconds till methi dana turns brown.
6. Add onion. Cook till soft.
7. Add the powdered dhania and red chillies and stir for ½ minute.
8. Add the chopped ginger and green chilli.
9. Add tomatoes and stir for about 5-7 minutes on low heat till oil separates.
10. Add tomato puree. Mix well.
11. Add salt, baby corns and capsicum. Cook for 2-3 minutes.
12. Mix in the shredded ginger. Serve hot.

Lazeez Aloo Matar

Serves 4

4 small sized potatoes - boiled
1½ tbsp til (sesame seeds)
¾ tsp jeera (cumin seeds)
3 tbsp oil
1 large onion - chopped very finely
4-5 cashews - split into halves
10-15 kishmish - soaked in water
¾ cup boiled or frozen peas
1 tsp salt, or to taste
¼ tsp haldi
½ tsp garam masala
½ tsp red chilli powder
½ tsp amchoor
2-3 tbsp chopped coriander
2 green chillies - slit lengthwise

1. Boil potatoes in salted water until just tender. They should feel soft when a knife is inserted. Do not over cook. (You may also microwave the potatoes if you wish, 4 potatoes would take about 4 minutes on full power, or pressure cook the potatoes for a quicker subzi).
2. Peel and cut each potato widthwise into 2 equal halves.
3. Heat oil. Add til and jeera. Wait till the til (sesame seeds) starts changing colour.
4. Add onions. Cook until onions turn light brown.
5. Add kaju. Stir-fry for a minute. Add kishmish.
6. Add salt, haldi, garam masala, red chilli powder and amchoor. Mix.
7. Add green chillies and fresh coriander. Cook for 1 minute.
8. Add the potatoes. Stir-fry gently for about 3 minutes on low heat, taking care not to break the potatoes. Keep them spaced apart and do not stir too much, so that they turn crisp.
9. Add 2-3 tbsp water.
10. Finally, add peas. Mix gently. Cook for 2 minutes stirring occasionally. Remove from fire. Serve hot.

Tawa Paneer

A unique preparation of cottage cheese cooked on a tawa.

Serves 4

MARINATE FOR 15 MINUTES
400 gms paneer (cottage cheese) - cut into 1½" cubes
½ tsp red chilli powder
½ tsp haldi
½ tsp salt
1 tsp chaat masala

MASALA
½ tsp jeera (cumin seeds)
½ tsp ajwain seeds (carom seeds)
1 large onion - chopped
3 tsp garlic paste
2 green chillies - chopped
2 tsp dhania (coriander) powder
½ tsp red chilli powder
½ tsp salt, or to taste
1 large tomato - chopped
1 capsicum - chopped
¼ tsp garam masala
¼ tsp shah jeera (black cumin)

1. Cut paneer into big, thick pieces. Sprinkle red chilli powder, haldi, salt and chaat masala. Mix well to coat both sides of paneer with the powdered masalas. Keep the marinated paneer aside for 15 minutes.
2. Heat 2 tbsp oil on a non stick tawa or a pan. Shallow fry the paneer on the tawa, turning sides, till light browned on all sides.
3. For the masala, heat 3 tbsp oil. When oil is hot, add ajwain and jeera. Let jeera turn golden.
4. Add the chopped onions and stir till golden.
5. Reduce heat. Add garlic paste, green chillies, coriander powder, red chilli powder, and salt. Fry on medium heat for a few seconds.
6. Add chopped tomatoes. Stir fry for 5-7 minutes till the oil separates. Keep aside.
7. Mix in the fried paneer, capsicum, garam masala, shah jeera. Mix and cook for 1-2 minutes. Serve hot.

Achaari Karele

Serves 4-6

½ kg small karelas (bitter gourd) - peeled, slit & deseeded
1 tsp salt
2 tbsp (a lemon sized ball) imli (tamarind)
3 tbsp plus 3 tbsp (6 tbsp) oil
1 tsp saunf and 1 tsp jeera - crushed slightly on a chakla-belan
¼ tsp kalonji (onion seeds)
¼ tsp methi daana (fenugreek seeds)
¼ tsp sarson
3 onions - grated or chopped very finely
6-8 flakes garlic - crushed, 2 green chillies - deseeded & chopped
½ tsp salt
½ tsp chilli powder
2 tsp dhania (coriander) powder
¼ tsp haldi
1 small raw mango - peeled & grated (¼ cup) or 1 tsp amchoor
6-8 small baby onions - peel and give 2 cross slits
some chaat masala

1. Boil 4 cups water with 1 tsp salt and imli. Add peeled and deseeded karelas. Boil on medium heat for 7-10 minutes or till soft. Strain. Keep aside.
2. Collect seeds - saunf, jeera, kalonji, methi daana and sarson together. Heat 3 tbsp oil in a pan. Add the collected seeds and stir for a few seconds till methi daana turns golden brown.
3. Add onion and cook till light pink in colour. Add garlic and green chillies. Cook further for ½ minute.
4. Add salt, red chilli powder and dhania powder. Add the raw mango or amchoor and cook till dry. Remove from heat and keep the filling aside to cool.
5. Fill the boiled karela with the prepared onion mixture.
6. Heat the remaining 3 tbsp oil in a big, heavy bottomed pan or kadhai. Place each karela carefully in oil. Turn a little to coat with oil. Then shift to the side. Add all the karelas. Keep them side by side and not overlapping each other. Cook on low heat for 10-15 minutes stirring in-between till karelas turn golden brown on all sides.
7. Add whole onions and cook further for 5 minutes. Sprinkle chat masala. Remove from fire and serve hot.

Gobi Mussallam

Picture on facing page   *Serves 8*

2 very small whole cauliflowers
¼ cup boiled peas - to garnish

GRIND TOGETHER TO A PASTE
2 small onions
4 tomatoes
1" piece ginger
1 green chilli

OTHER INGREDIENTS FOR MASALA
4 tbsp oil, ½ tsp shah jeera
½ tsp red chilli powder, 1 tsp dhania (coriander) powder
½ tsp amchoor, 1 tsp garam masala
¼ cup milk, salt to taste
1 tsp tandoori masala, 2-3 chhoti illaichi (green cardamom) - seeds crushed
50 gms paneer - grated (½ cup), 3 tbsp chopped coriander

1. Remove stem of cauliflower. Boil 5-6 cups water with 2 tsp salt. Put the whole cauliflower in it and leave it in hot water for 10 minutes. Remove from water and wash. Wipe dry with a towel.
2. Heat 5-6 tbsp oil in a large kadhai. Put both cauliflowers with flower side in oil. Cover and cook on medium flame, stirring occasionally till the cauliflowers turns golden and get cooked. Remove from oil and keep aside.
3. Heat 4 tbsp oil. Add shah jeera. After a minute, add the ground onion-tomato paste and cook till dry and oil separates. Reduce flame. Add red chilli powder, dhania, amchoor and garam masala. Cook for 1 minute.
4. Keeping the flame low, add milk stirring continuously. Stir for 2-3 minutes to get a thick masala. Add salt to taste. Insert a little masala in between the florets of the fried cauliflower. Insert from the backside also.
5. To the remaining masala, add enough water to get a gravy. Boil. Simmer for 5-7 minutes till slightly thick. Add tandoori masala, chhoti illaichi, paneer and coriander. Boil. Add a little salt. Cook for 1 minute. Remove from fire.
6. To serve, arrange the cauliflowers on a platter. Add 3-4 tbsp water to the masala to make it a little thin. Boil. Pour over the arranged cauliflowers. Heat in a preheated oven. Sprinkle some boiled peas on it and on the sides. Serve.

Dal Makhani : Recipe on page 56, Gobi Mussallam ➤

Makai Palak

Serves 4

500 gms paalak (spinach)
1 cup cooked corn kernels
1" piece ginger - grated
3 tbsp oil or ghee
2 moti illaichi (black cardamoms)
1" stick dalchini (cinnamon)
5-6 flakes garlic - crushed to a rough paste
2 onions - finely sliced
3 tomatoes - chopped
3/4 tsp haldi (turmeric powder)
1 tsp dhania powder (ground coriander)
½ tsp red chilli powder
½ tsp garam masala
1 tsp salt, or to taste

1. Boil whole fresh corn or frozen corn kernels with ¼ tsp haldi, 2 tsp sugar and 1 tsp salt to get soft, yellow, sweetish corn. If using tinned corn, simply drain the water and use.
2. Heat oil. Reduce heat. Add moti illaichi and dalchini. Wait for a minute.
3. Add garlic and cook till it starts to change colour.
4. Add onions and stir fry till golden. Reduce heat.
5. Add haldi powder, dhania powder, chilli powder, garam masala and salt. Mix well on low heat for a minute.
6. Add ginger. Stir for a few seconds.
7. Add corn. Stir fry for 2-3 minutes.
8. Add spinach. Continue cooking, without covering, for about 10 minutes, till the spinach gets wilted and is well blended with the corn.
9. Add tomatoes and stir fry for 3-4 minutes. Garnish with ginger match sticks and serve hot with chapattis.

Paneer Amravati

Onion and coconut shreds coat paneer fingers in a South Indian style.

Serves 4-6

200 gm paneer - cut into thin fingers
4 onions - 2 grated and 2 sliced
½ cup curry leaves
6 tbsp oil
1½ tsp brown small rai (mustard seeds)
¼ cup fresh coconut - grated finely
1¼ tsp salt, or to taste
3 tbsp lemon juice (juice of 1 large lemon)
a pinch of tandoori red colour
1 tbsp cashews - crushed

RED CHILLI PASTE
4 dry, Kashmiri red chillies - deseeded and soaked in warm water for 10 minutes
1" piece ginger
3 tbsp curd
2 tsp dhania powder
2-3 laung (cloves), 6-7 saboot kali mirch (peppercorns)

1. Grate 2 onions.
2. Cut the other 2 onions into halves. Then cut each half widthwise into semi-rings to get thin strips of onion.
3. Scrape the brown skin of a small piece of coconut and grate finely to get ¼ cup grated coconut.
4. Drain the soaked red chillies. Add all other ingredients of the paste and grind to a smooth paste using a little water for grinding.
5. Heat oil. Add rai. Let it splutter for a minute.
6. Add grated onions and curry leaves. Cook till onions turn light brown.
7. Add onion slices and cook for 3-4 minutes till soft.
8. Add coconut and cook on low heat for 5 minutes till crisp. Keep it spread out while cooking.
9. Add red chilli paste and cashews. Stir fry for 2-3 minutes.
10. Add colour and salt.
11. Add 1 cup water. Boil.
12. Add paneer and mix well.
13. Cover and cook on low heat for 5 minutes, stirring occasionally.
14. Add lemon juice and mix well. Serve hot.

Bhindi Dakshini

Serves 4

250 gm bhindi

MASALA
2 tbsp oil
1 tsp channa dal
1 tsp urad dal
½ tsp jeera (cumin seeds)
½ tsp sarson (mustard seeds)
2 dry, red chillies - broken into pieces
10-12 curry pattas
1 green chilli - deseeded & chopped
1 large onion - chopped
2 tomatoes - chopped
½ tsp dhania (coriander) powder
¼ tsp chilli powder
¾ tsp salt, or to taste
pinch of haldi
3 tbsp thick curd - beat till smooth
grated fresh coconut for garnish, optional

1. Wash bhindi and wipe dry. Cut the tip of the head of each bhindi, leaving the pointed end as it is. Now cut the bhindi vertically from the middle making 2 smaller pieces from each bhindi. Heat oil in a kadhai and deep fry the bhindi on medium heat in 2 batches. Do not over fry the bhindi, it should retain it's green colour. Drain on a paper napkin. Keep aside.
2. Heat 2 tbsp oil in a pan. Reduce heat. Add both the dals and stir for a few seconds till dals change colour.
3. Add jeera, sarson and dry, red chillies.
4. Stir and add curry patta, green chilli and onions. Cook till onion turns light brown.
5. Add the tomatoes and cook for 2 minutes till soft.
6. Add the dry masalas - dhania powder, red chilli powder, salt and haldi. Bhuno the masalas for 2 minutes.
7. Add ¼ cup water and the fried bhindi. Cover and cook for 1 minute.
8. Add curd. Cook on medium heat till the water from the curd evaporates.
9. Stir for 3-4 minutes till the masala coats the bhindi. Garnish with grated coconut if you like. Serve with chappati and raita.

Katliyaan Aloo

Serves 4

6 medium potatoes - cut into ¼" thick round slices
2 medium onions - sliced
3 tbsp oil
½ tsp jeera (cumin seeds)
½ tsp saunf (ani seeds)
¼ tsp kalonji (onion seeds)
¼ tsp rai (mustard seeds)
a pinch methi daana (fenugreek seeds)
2 dried, red chillies - crushed
4 flakes garlic - crushed
½" piece ginger - cut into thin match sticks
a few curry leaves
½ tsp haldi
salt to taste
1 tsp chaat masala
1 tbsp coriander - chopped
1 fresh red chilli - deseeded & cut into thin match sticks
1 green chilli - deseeded & cut into thin match sticks

1. Peel, wash and cut potatoes into ¼" thick round slices.
2. Heat oil in a kadhai or a non stick wok.
3. Reduce heat slightly, add jeera, saunf, kalonji, rai and methi daana. Fry for ½ minute till the saunf starts changing colour.
4. Add garlic, ginger, red chillies and curry leaves, bhuno for 1 minute.
5. Add onions, bhuno until onions turn light golden. Add haldi. Stir.
6. Add potatoes and salt. Mix well.
7. Add coriander, fresh red and green chillies, stir until well mixed.
8. Reduce to very low heat, cover tightly with a lid, and cook for 10-12 minutes or until the potatoes are tender. Uncover and add chaat masala. Adjust the seasonings.
9. Transfer to a serving platter and serve hot.

Arbi Mumtaaz

Picture on page 87   *Serves 4*

½ kg arbi (calocassia)
2 onions - cut into rings
½" piece ginger - chopped finely
2-3 green chillies - cut into long pieces
2 tomatoes - chopped
¼ tsp haldi
½ tsp ajwain (carom seeds)
½ tsp jeera (cumin seeds)
1 tsp dhania (coriander) powder
½ tsp salt, or to taste
½ tsp red chilli powder
½ tsp amchoor (dried mango powder)
½ cup chopped coriander

1. Pressure cook arbi with 3 cups water with 2 tsp salt to give one whistle. Keep on low flame for 4-5 minutes. Do not over boil. Peel and flatten each piece between the palms.
2. Heat 2 cups oil in a kadhai for frying. Put 4-5 pieces of flattened arbi at one time in oil. Fry till golden brown. Remove from oil. Keep aside.
3. Heat 2 tbsp oil in a clean kadhai. Reduce flame. Add ajwain and jeera. Cook till jeera turns golden.
4. Add onion rings and cook till soft. Add haldi and mix.
5. Add tomatoes and cook for 2 minutes till soft. Add ginger and stir for a minute.
6. Add chilli powder, amchoor, salt and dhania powder. Stir to mix well. Add 2-3 tbsp water. Boil.
7. Add fried arbi. Mix well. Add hara dhania and green chillies. Stir fry for 1-2 minutes. Serve.

Note: If the arbi is not boiled in salted water, add a little extra salt.

BAKED DISHES

Potatoes Baked in Mustard Sauce

Serves 4

4 round potatoes - boiled in salted water & peeled
½ cup boiled corn (fresh corn should be boiled with a pinch of haldi)
1 tbsp butter
½ onion - finely chopped
1 green chilli - deseeded and chopped finely, 2 tbsp finely chopped coriander
¼ tsp salt, ¼ tsp freshly ground pepper or to taste
50 gms cheese

MUSTARD SAUCE
1 tsp mustard powder
2 tbsp butter, 2 tbsp maida (plain flour)
1 tej patta (bay leaf)
1½ cups milk
½ cup cream
½ tsp salt, or to taste
¼ tsp pepper

1. Half the potatoes widthwise. Scoop out a little with the back of a teaspoon, leaving a ¼" wall. Sprinkle some salt and pepper on the potatoes. Keep aside.
2. Melt 1 tbsp butter in a clean kadhai. Add onion and green chilli . Stir fry till light golden. Add salt, freshly ground pepper & coriander. Add the corn. Toss well for a couple of minutes. Remove from fire.
3. Stuff the filling into the potato shells. Keep the left over filling aside.
4. To prepare the mustard sauce, melt 2 tbsp butter. Add tej patta.
5. Add mustard powder and maida. Cook on low heat for 1 minute.
6. Add milk and mix well. Cook, stirring continuously till the sauce turns slightly thick and coats the back of the spoon.
7. Remove from heat and add the cream. Add salt and pepper to taste. Remove the bay leaf.
8. Pour some mustard sauce (¼ of it) at the base of the serving dish.
9. Slice just a little from the bottom of each stuffed potato, so that it can sit upright in the dish.
10. Arrange the potatoes and spread the rest of the sauce over the potatoes. Sprinkle the left over corn filling.
11. Grate cheese on top and bake till cheese turns brown. Serve hot.

Sweet & Sour Cabbage

A Chinese style of baking cabbage.

Serves 8

1 medium cabbage (about ½ kg) - cut into 1" squares
4 tomatoes
½ cup grated carrot (1 big)
3 tbsp oil
2 tbsp cornflour
1 cup water
2 tbsp vinegar
1 tbsp soya sauce
1 tbsp sugar
2 tsp salt, or to taste

1. Put tomatoes in boiling water for 3-4 minutes. Remove from water and remove the skin and chop.
2. Heat oil and fry the grated carrot and chopped tomatoes for about 5 minutes.
3. Blend in a mixer. Remove from mixer to a bowl.
4. To the tomatoes add vinegar, sugar, soya sauce and salt and mix well.
5. Mix cornflour in 1 cup of water and add to the tomato mixture. Keep it on fire and cook till the mixture is thick and translucent.
6. Cut cabbage into 1" squares.
7. In a greased glass baking dish put the cabbage pieces.
8. Pour over the sweet and sour sauce. Mix gently.
9. Bake in a preheated oven for 20-25 minutes or till the cabbage is done.

Florets in Broccoli Sauce

Serves 5-6

200 gm (½ of a medium) cauliflower, 150 gm (1 small flower) broccoli
1 large carrot - finely chopped
juice of ½ lemon
2 tbsp butter
3-4 flakes garlic - crushed, 1 onion - cut into half and then into rings
¼ tsp salt
¼ tsp peppercorns (saboot kali mirch) - crushed
2 tbsp grated cheese

BROCCOLI SAUCE
3 tbsp butter
1 tiny flower of broccoli - scraped with a knife from the top to get 1 cup very fine
pieces (like crumbs) of broccoli (do not use the stalk)
3 tbsp plain flour (maida)
3¼ cups milk, 2 tbsp grated cheese
¾ tsp salt and ¼ tsp pepper, or to taste

1. Cut cauliflower and broccoli into medium florets with small stalks.
2. Boil 5-6 cups water with 2 tsp salt, 1 tsp sugar and juice of ½ lemon. Add florets and carrots to boiling water. When a proper boils comes, remove from fire. Leave vegetables in hot water for 2 minutes. Drain. Do not over cook. Refresh in cold water. Strain. Pat dry on a clean kitchen towel or a paper napkin.
3. Pick up the cauliflower and broccoli florets. Heat butter. Add garlic and onions. Cook till onions turn golden. Add both the florets. Add salt and pepper. Saute, stirring very little, till brown specs appear on the cauliflower. Transfer to an oven proof serving dish.
4. Sprinkle carrots over the florets in the dish. Sprinkle 2 tbsp cheese and some crushed peppercorns on the vegetables.
5. To prepare the sauce, melt butter in a heavy bottomed pan. Add broccoli. Stir for 2 minutes. Add flour. Cook on slow fire for 1-2 minutes. Add milk gradually, stirring continuously. Stir till it boils. Cook for 2-3 minutes. Do not make it too thick. Add 2 tbsp cheese. Add salt and pepper to taste. Remove from fire.
6. Spread the white sauce over the vegetables. Bake at 200°C/475°F for 20 minutes till light brown. Serve immediately.

Quick Casserole

Serves 4

4 small brinjals (long variety) - sliced
4 potatoes - boiled
2 tomatoes - sliced thinly
2 tbsp chopped coriander
4 tbsp butter
salt, pepper to taste
oil to fry
50-100 gm cheese - grated

1. Slice brinjals into thin rounds. Shallow fry in oil in a pan, till light brown in colour.
2. Boil potatoes carefully. Do not over boil. Peel and slice them. Keep aside.
3. Melt butter in a small pan.
4. Grease a baking dish. Spread half to the brinjals. Sprinkle a little salt and pepper.
5. Spread 3 tbsp grated cheese on the brinjals.
6. Spread half of the potatoes on the cheese. Pour half the melted butter on the potatoes.
7. Arrange a layer with a half of the tomatoes. Sprinkle salt and pepper.
8. Repeat the layers using the left over brinjals, then a sprinkling of cheese and then a layer of tomatoes.
9. Arrange a final layer of potatoes, slightly overlapping each other. Pour melted butter carefully on all the slices. Sprinkle some chopped coriander.
10. Bake in a preheated oven at 200°C/400°F till potatoes turn golden.
11. Garnish with freshly chopped coriander.

Corn & Coriander Bake

Check that the corn kernels are really sweet to get a sweet & salty dish.

Serves 4

SAUCE
1 cup tinned corn or niblets 1 large corn, see note
2½ cups milk
2 tbsp butter - softened, 2 tbsp flour (maida), ½ tsp salt, ¼ tsp pepper
2 tbsp grated cheese
3-4 tbsp chopped fresh coriander, preferably the stalks

BASE LAYER
4 slices bread
2 tbsp butter, ¼ tsp salt and ¼ tsp red chilli flakes
2 tbsp grated cheese

TOPPING
2 tbsp grated cheese
2 tbsp melted butter

1. For the base layer, break the bread slices into small pieces. Grind in a mixer to get fresh bread crumbs.
2. Melt 2 tbsp butter in a pan. Add the fresh bread crumbs, salt and red chilli flakes. Saute for 5 minutes. Remove from fire.
3. Spread these buttered bread crumbs at the base of a greased oven proof dish. Sprinkle 2 tbsp grated cheese on the bread. Keep aside.
4. For the sauce, heat butter. Add flour. Cook on low heat for 1 minute.
5. Add the milk, stirring continuously. Add ½ tsp salt, ¼ tsp pepper and stir till it comes to a boil.
6. When the sauce is thick, add the cheese and mix well.
7. Mix in the corn and coriander. Remove from fire.
8. Pour the mixture over the bread crumbs in the dish.
9. Sprinkle grated cheese and pour some melted butter on it.
10. Bake in a preheated oven at 180°C/350°F/Gas mark 4 for 25-30 minutes or until golden brown. Serve.

Note: If using fresh or frozen corn, boil it in 3 cups water with a pinch of haldi, 1 tsp salt and 1 tbsp sugar added to the water to get sweet corn niblets.

Crispy Potato Bake

You will never imagine how tasty potatoes can be!

Serves 6

4 big (½ kg) potatoes - peeled and cut into very thin slices
4-5 tbsp melted butter
1 cup grated cheese (100 gm)
1 cup cream
1 tsp salt and ½ tsp pepper

1. Wash the potatoes. Peel and slice them very thinly.
2. Grease a glass oven proof dish and put a layer with some slices of potatoes, sprinkle cheese on them and finally pour some melted butter.
3. Repeat layers of potato slices, cheese and butter till all the potatoes are used up.
4. Mix 1 tsp salt and ½ tsp pepper in 1 cup cream.
5. Pour the cream on the potatoes.
6. Sprinkle cheese.
7. Crush 5-6 peppercorns and sprinkle on the cheese.
8. Cover with aluminium foil and bake in a preheated oven at 180°C/350°F/Gas mark 4 for about 60 minutes till the potatoes are tender and crisp. Check the potatoes before removing the dish from the oven. Serve.

Spinach Vegetable Bake

Serves 4

350 gm (½ bundle) paalak (spinach)
1 tsp garlic (6-7 flakes) - crushed & chopped, 1-2 green chillies - chopped
1 tbsp butter
salt & pepper to taste
2½ cups milk
1½ tbsp cornflour, 1 tbsp maida
1 tej patta (bay leaf), 1" stick dalchini (cinnamon)
2 cups finely chopped mixed vegetables (½ carrot, ¼ of a cauliflower, ¼ cup
shelled peas, 5-6 beans)
¾ cup mozzarella or pizza cheese - grated, 1 tbsp butter
1 tsp salt, ½ tsp pepper and ¼ tsp mustard, or to taste
¼ cup dried bread crumbs

1. Heat oven 200°C. Discard the stems of spinach and wash leaves well under running water. Finely chop the spinach leaves. Pat dry the leaves.
2. Heat butter. Add garlic and green chillies. Stir and add the spinach. Cook till water evaporates. Sprinkle some salt and pepper. Remove from heat.
3. In a small oven proof dish, spread the cooked spinach. Sprinkle 2 tbsp grated cheese.
4. Heat 2 cups of milk in a heavy bottomed sauce pan with a bay leaf and cinnamon stick. Bring the milk to a boil and add the chopped vegetables. Reduce heat and simmer covered till done.
5. Meanwhile dissolve cornflour and maida in the remaining ½ cup of milk.
6. When vegetables get just cooked (do not make them too soft), add the dissolved cornflour and maida to the vegetables. Cook till sauce thickens.
7. Add 4 tbsp grated cheese, butter, salt, pepper and mustard. Remove from heat. Discard the bay leaf and cinnamon stick.
8. Pour the cooked vegetables on the spinach and level with a spoon. Sprinkle bread crumbs. Sprinkle left over cheese. Bake for 8 minutes at 210°C. Serve with buttered toasts or bread buns.

Note: To make crumbs, tear bread slices into small pieces and microwave these for 3-4 minutes on high power, mixing once in between to turn sides. Let it stand for 2 minutes to dry out. Grind in a mixer to get crumbs.

Cauliflower & Cottage Cheese Bake

Serves 4

100 gm paneer - cut into ¼" pieces
1 cauliflower - cut into ½" florets (2 cups)
1 tbsp butter
salt & freshly ground pepper
50 gm mozzarella cheese - grated
2½ tbsp butter
1 tsp oregano
3 tbsp maida
2 cups milk
½ tsp red chilli flakes
½ tsp mustard
½ tsp peppercorns - crushed
¾ tsp salt, or to taste

1. Heat oven to 200°C.
2. Boil 4-5 cups water with 1 tsp salt and juice of ½ lemon. Add cauliflower. Boil for only 2-3 minutes, keeping it crisp - tender. Strain and wipe dry.
3. Heat butter in a kadhai. Saute cauliflower for 2-3 minutes till brown specs appear. Add some salt and pepper. Transfer to a greased oven proof dish.
4. Sprinkle some salt & coarsely ground peppercorns on paneer. Sprinkle paneer on the cauliflower in the dish.
5. For sauce, heat butter. Add flour. Mix and add oregano. Cook on low heat for 1 minute. Add milk and stir. Add mustard, salt, pepper and red chilli flakes. Stir continuously till the sauce starts coating the back of the spoon.
6. Remove from fire. Add ½ of the grated cheese. Pour sauce over the paneer.
7. Sprinkle chopped parsley or coriander and left over cheese. Bake for 7-8 minutes in a hot oven at 210°C till cheese melts.

Corn with Asparagus

Serves 8

1 cup tinned, cooked or frozen corn kernels
10-12 stalks of fresh or tinned asparagus
2 carrots - cut into small cubes
100 gm mozzarella cheese - grated

HERBED WHITE SAUCE
2½ tbsp flour
2½ tbsp butter
2½ cups milk
1 tsp salt and ¾ tsp pepper, or to taste
1 tsp oregano

1. If using fresh asparagus, snip 1½" from the lower end. If the asparagus is tough, you may also need to peel the lower stem with a peeler thinly. If tender, just snip the ends. Cut the asparagus into 2" pieces. To boil asparagus, boil 2 cups water with 1 tsp salt and ½ tsp sugar in a pan. Add asparagus and carrots. Cook uncovered on low heat for 3-4 minutes till tender by feeling the stem of the asparagus. Remove from water and drain. If using tinned asparagus, there is no need to boil it. Keep vegetables aside.

2. For the sauce, melt the butter & stir in the flour. Stir for 1 minute. Gradually add the milk and bring to a boil stirring continuously. Keep on low heat for 3-4 minutes.

3. Keeping aside 4-5 upper portions of the asparagus for garnishing, add the rest of the asparagus to the white sauce. Add corn and carrots also to the sauce. Cook on low heat for 3-4 minutes till thick. Add salt and pepper to taste. Remove from fire. Add half of the grated cheese and oregano. Mix well.

4. Grease a baking dish and put the corn-carrot-asparagus mixture in it.

5. Cover with the remaining cheese. Garnish with the remaining asparagus pieces.

6. Bake in a hot oven at 200°C for 20 minutes or until golden. Serve hot.

Vegetable au Gratin

Serves 8   *Picture on page 2*

WHITE SAUCE
4 tbsp butter
4 tbsp maida (plain flour)
3 cups milk
salt, pepper to taste
1 tbsp tomato ketchup

VEGETABLES
10-15 french beans - cut diagonally into small pieces
2 carrots - cut into small cubes
½ small cauliflower - cut into small flowerets
½ cup shelled peas
1 medium potato - cut into small cubes
½ small (250 gm) ghiya (bottle gourd) - cut into small cubes

TOPPING
¼ cup bread crumbs
1 firm tomato - sliced

1. To prepare the sauce, heat butter in a clean heavy bottomed pan, on low flame.
2. When butter melts, add the flour and mix stirring continuously on low flame for 1 minute. Do not let the colour change.
3. Remove from fire and add milk. Mix well. Return to fire and stir continuously till the sauce becomes thick.
4. Add salt, pepper and tomato ketchup to it. Keep sauce aside.
5. Wash vegetables & pressure cook with 1 tsp salt with ¼ cup water, till the hissing sound starts. Remove from fire before the whistle. Strain vegetables. Cool.
6. Mix steamed vegetables with the prepared sauce. Add salt if required.
7. Transfer to a shallow borosil dish. Arrange tomato slices over it. Sprinkle bread crumbs. Bake in a hot oven at 240°C/475°F, till golden brown for about 35 minutes. Remove from the oven and serve hot.

Bread & Cheese Bake

A good dish when you have nothing substantial in the house! Just bread & cheese is enough.

Serves 6-8

6 bread slices
1½ cups grated cheese (150 gm)
3 tbsp butter - softened
1½ cups milk
2 tbsp flour (maida)
½ tsp mustard powder or paste
½ tsp salt and ½ tsp freshly ground pepper

1. Heat 2 tbsp of butter. Add the flour and stir for a minute on low heat. Add milk stirring continuously. Cook till thick.
2. Season with salt, pepper and mustard. Keep white sauce aside.
3. Butter the bread slices nicely and crumble it with your hands.
4. Grease an oven proof dish and spread a layer using ½ of the fresh bread crumbs.
5. Sprinkle 1/3 of the cheese on the bread.
6. Repeat the bread layer using all the left over bread.
7. Sprinkle half the cheese.
8. Pour the cheese sauce to cover nicely. Sprinkle the remaining cheese and top with 4-5 freshly crushed peppercorns.
9. Bake in a preheated oven at 180°C/350°F/Gas mark 4 for 30 minutes.

Malai Khumb Matar : Recipe on page 53 ➢
Arbi Mumtaz : Recipe on page 74 ➢

Baby Corn & Mushroom Au Gratin

Serves 5-6

100 gm baby corns, fresh or tinned - sliced into 2 lengthways
125 gm (12-15) small sized mushrooms (fresh or tinned) - cut the stem into round
slices and the head into 2 pieces horizontally
1 carrot - peeled and cut into small cubes
1 onion - finely sliced
2 tbsp butter, 3-4 tbsp grated cheese, optional

HERBED WHITE SAUCE
2 tbsp butter, 2 tbsp plain flour (maida), 2½ cups milk
3/4 tsp salt, ¼ tsp crushed peppercorns, ¼ tsp paprika or red chilli flakes
3 tbsp finely chopped herb - mint or parsley or dill (soye) or coriander
¼ tsp grated nutmeg (jaiphal)

1. For fresh baby corns and carrots, boil 3 cups water with 1 tsp salt. Add baby corns and carrots. Boil for 1-2 minutes, after the first boil. Remove vegetables with a slotted spoon. If you are using tinned baby corns, there is no need to boil them.
2. For mushrooms, add 2 tsp lemon juice to the above water and boil again. Add mushrooms and boil for 1-2 minutes on medium flame. Drain. Wipe dry.
3. Melt 2 tbsp butter in a nonstick pan and add onions and stir fry till brown. Remove from butter. Keep aside. Saute mushrooms in the same pan in the remaining butter for 3 minutes till light brown and dry. Remove from pan. Keep aside. In the same pan, saute the baby corns and carrots for 2 minutes till brown specs appear on the corns.
4. To prepare herbed white sauce, melt 2 tbsp butter in a clean pan. Add any herb (mint or coriander or dill or parsley). Stir for 1 minute. Add flour and cook on low flame for 1-2 minutes. Remove from fire.
5. Gradually add milk, stirring continuously. Return to fire. Boil. Simmer for 2 minutes. Add salt, pepper and nutmeg. Remove from fire.
6. To assemble, grease an oven proof dish. Spread 3-4 tbsp white sauce first at the bottom of the dish. Spread a few fried onions.
7. Keeping aside 4 baby corn pieces for garnishing, spread the rest of baby corns, and all the carrots and mushrooms over the onions. Cover with herbed sauce. Sprinkle onions. Sprinkle cheese. Arrange baby corns in one corner to garnish. Bake at 220°C for 15 minutes till golden. Serve hot.

Italian Tomatoes

Whole blanched tomatoes in a delicious sauce make a good accompaniment to the main meal.

Serves 6

6 medium sized tomatoes - blanched
2 tbsp olive oil
1 tsp ginger paste
1 tsp garlic paste
1 tsp sugar
¾ cup tomato sauce
2 tbsp chilli sauce
1 tbsp oregano
½ cup grated cheese
¾ tsp salt
¼ tsp pepper

1. To blanch tomatoes, put them in hot water for 3-4 minutes and remove the skin. Keep whole tomatoes aside.
2. Heat oil and fry the ginger and garlic paste.
3. Add tomato sauce, chilli sauce, sugar, salt and pepper.
4. Place the whole tomatoes in an oven proof dish and pour over the sauce over them. Sprinkle oregano and grated cheese.
5. Bake in a preheated oven at 180°C/350°F/Gas mark 4 for 25-30 minutes.

Cheesy Baked Noodles

Serves 4

BOIL TOGETHER
50 gms (½ packet) chow noodles - boiled (1¼ cups)
1 tsp oil
6 cups water
1 tsp salt

CHEESE SAUCE
4 tbsp butter, 4 tbsp maida (plain flour)
2½ cups milk (cold)
1 tsp salt or to taste
½ tsp pepper, 25 gms (1 cube) cheese
2 tbsp chopped coriander

TOPPING
½ tomato
½ capsicum
1 cube (25 gm) cheese
1 tsp butter

1. Boil 6 cups water with salt and oil in a large pan. Put ½ packet of noodles into the boiling water. Open noodles with a fork. Boil on high flame for 3 minutes. Remove from fire. Strain the noodles. Add fresh water and strain once again. Keep adding cold water and straining till the noodles are no longer hot. Keep them in the strainer for 10 minutes. Sprinkle 1 tsp oil and gently mix. Keep aside.
2. To prepare the sauce, heat butter on low flame in a clean heavy bottomed pan. When butter melts, add the flour and mix stirring continuously on low flame for 1 minute. Remove from fire and add milk. Mix well. Return to fire and stir continuously till the sauce becomes thick and coats the spoon. Keeping the flame low, add salt and pepper. Add coriander.
3. Grate one cube (25 gms) of cheese and mix with the hot sauce.
4. Mix the boiled noodles with the sauce. Add more salt and pepper if required. Remove from fire.
5. Grease a shallow borosil dish (2" high) and transfer the noodle mix in it.
6. Bake in a preheated oven at 200°C /400°F for ½ hour or till the top turns brown. Remove from oven. Grate a cube of cheese over the noodles.
7. Remove pulp of tomato and seeds of capsicum. Cut into very thin ½" long pieces and sprinkle over the grated cheese. Dot with butter at 4-5 places.
8. Put the noodles back into the oven. Bake for 5-7 minutes. Serve hot.

Stuffed Cabbage Rolls

A very unusual baked dish. The sweet and sour sauce makes the cabbage really amazing! Must give it a try.

Serves 6-8

8 outer large cabbage leaves
2 onions - chopped
1½ cups paneer - crumbled (200 gm)
1½ cups tomato puree
1 tsp vinegar
2 flakes garlic - crushed
4 tbsp oil
1 tsp sugar
1 tsp salt, ½ tsp pepper

1. To break the outer leaves, cut leaves from the stalk end and gently pull from the cut end to get a whole leaf.
2. Boil 6-7 cups of water in a large pan with 2 tsp of salt and 1 tsp sugar. Add cabbage leaves to the boiling water. Cook cabbage in boiling salted water for 3-4 minutes. Drain and cool.
3. Heat 2 tbsp oil. Add onion and cook till golden. Add the paneer and mix well. Add ½ tsp salt & ¼ tsp pepper to taste. Stir for 1 minute and remove from fire.
4. To make the sauce, heat 2 tbsp oil and fry the garlic till it just changes colour. Add the tomato puree, vinegar, sugar, ¾ tsp salt and ½ tsp pepper. Cook for 2 minutes. Remove from fire and check seasonings. Keep aside.
5. Divide the paneer mixture into 8 portions. Place one portion of paneer in the centre of a cabbage leaf. Spread it along the width of the leaf and then roll. Cut the hard end of the leaf. Pierce a toothpick on the hard central vein of the leaf.
6. Place the rolls close together in a greased baking dish.
7. Pour the sauce over.
8. Cover and bake in a preheated oven at 180°C/350°F/Gas mark 4 for 25-30 minutes.

PASTA
&
CONTINENTAL DISHES

Spaghetti Casserole

Spaghetti topped with a red tomato based sauce.

Serves 4-5

200 gm spaghetti - boiled (5 cups)
2 tbsp olive oil, 1 tbsp butter
2 spring onions - cut into slices or ½ onion - chopped and ½ capsicum - cut into small thin fingers
salt, freshly ground pepper to taste, 2 tbsp cream or milk
30-50 gm of processed or parmesan cheese - grated

SAUCE
3-4 tbsp olive oil or any cooking oil, 6-7 flakes garlic - crushed
150-200 gm mushrooms - sliced, 1 capsicum - cut into ½" pieces
4 large tomatoes - blended to puree, ¼ cup (4 tbsp) tomato puree
¼ tsp chilli flakes, 1 tsp oregano, ½ tsp sugar, 1 tsp salt, or to taste

TOPPING
75-100 gm paneer - crumbled
100 gm mozzarella cheese - grated

1. Heat oven to 200°C.
2. Heat 7-8 cups of water in a large pan with 2 tsp salt and 2 tsp oil. Holding the bunch of spaghetti in the hand, gradually slide it into the boiling water. Cook uncovered for about 5 minutes or till done. Drain the cooked spaghetti and refresh under cold water.
3. While the spaghetti is boiling, prepare the sauce. Heat oil in a kadhai and add the garlic. Wait for about ½ minute.
4. Stir and add the mushrooms and capsicum. Saute for 1-2 minutes.
5. Add freshly pureed tomatoes. Cook till moisture of the tomatoes evaporates.
6. Add ready made tomato puree, chilli flakes, oregano, sugar, salt and pepper. Add ½ cup of water and bring to boil. Remove from heat.
7. To assemble, heat a clean pan with olive oil and butter. Add spring onions and stir for a few seconds.
8. Add the spaghetti and stir well to coat in butter and oil. Sprinkle salt and freshly ground pepper.
9. Add milk or cream and cheese. Mix and remove to an oven proof dish.
10. Pour the prepared sauce over it.
11. Top with crumbled paneer and grated mozzarella cheese. To serve, grill for 4-5 minutes. Serve hot.

Pasta with Mushrooms & Tomato Slices

A very quick, yet delightful recipe.

Picture on page 1   *Serves 6*

2 cups pasta (fussili, macaroni, penne or any other type)
100 gm mushrooms - chopped (1½ cups)
1 onion - chopped
4 tomatoes - blanched, peeled and cut into round slices
3 tbsp oil, 1 tbsp butter
¾ cup grated cheese, preferably mozzarella cheese
¾ cup cream (vijaya or fresh)
¼ tsp salt, ¼ tsp pepper

1. Boil pasta in 5-6 cups of water with 1 tsp of oil and 1 tsp salt for 10 minutes or until just tender. Drain and put in cold water. Strain and keep aside.
2. Heat 1 tbsp butter in pan. Add boiled pasta, ¼ tsp salt, ¼ tsp pepper and ¼ tsp red chilli flakes. Saute pasta for 2-3 minutes. Keep aside.
3. Heat the oil and fry the chopped onion until soft. Add mushrooms, ½ tsp salt and ½ tsp pepper and fry for 5 minutes. Keep aside.
4. To blanch tomatoes, put them in boiling water for 2 minutes. Remove from water immediately after 2 minutes. Cool. Peel the skin and cut them into round slices.
5. In a greased dish put a layer of pasta, top with onion and mushrooms. Cover with sliced tomatoes.
6. Lastly sprinkle half the cheese.
7. Mix cream with ¼ tsp salt and ¼ tsp pepper. Pour the cream over the tomatoes. Spread the cream all over with the back of a spoon.
8. Top with the remaining grated cheese.
9. Bake in a preheated oven at 200°C/400°F/Gas mark 6 for 15-20 minutes. Serve hot.

Peppery Aubergines

Delicious brinjals - must give it a try!

Serves 4

1 large (round) baingan (aubergine)
2 tbsp oil
5-6 flakes garlic - crushed
1 onion - cut into 4 pieces and separated
1 green capsicum - deseeded and cut into 1" cubes
1 tomato - deseeded & cubed
2 tbsp tomato sauce
1 tsp soya sauce
1 tsp Worcestershire sauce
½ tsp freshly ground pepper
½ tsp salt, or to taste

1. Wash and chop baingan into 2" cubes. Sprinkle 1 tsp salt and keep aside for 7-8 minutes in a colander (a big strainer with large holes, normally used for straining rice.) This salting is called degorging and removes the bitterness in the aubergines.
2. Meanwhile cut the onion into fours and open the layers of the onion. Cut capsicum into 1" pieces, deseed the tomato and cut into cubes. Keep aside. Peel and crush garlic. Keep aside.
3. Heat oil for frying in a kadhai.
4. Rinse the baingans with water nicely. Pat dry on a kitchen towel. Fry the baingans till brown. They should turn light brown and not remain whitish. Drain on paper napkins.
5. Heat 2 tbsp oil in a kadhai. Add garlic, stir add the onion and the capsicum. Saute for 1 minute.
6. Add the fried aubergines, cubed tomato and all the three sauces.
7. Add ½ tsp salt and freshly crushed peppercorns. Serve hot with garlic bread.

Penne with Basil

Picture on facing page   *Serves 4-6*

2 tbsp olive oil or butter
1 onion - finely chopped
2 garlic flakes - crushed
500 gm tomatoes - blanched in hot water, skinned & pureed till smooth
1 tsp dried oregano
1 tbsp tomato sauce
2 tbsp chopped fresh basil or mint or parsley
½ tsp sugar
1 tsp salt, or to taste
3 cups boiled penne or any other pasta (boil 2 cups raw pasta)
½ cup grated cheese (mozzarella) to sprinkle on top
some freshly ground pepper
a few basil leaves - put in chilled water to garnish

1. Heat oil. Add onion and garlic, cook until onions turn light brown.
2. Add tomatoes, oregano, tomato sauce, basil, salt and sugar, cook for 5 minutes, stirring occasionally. Keep sauce aside.
3. At serving time, melt 1 tbsp butter in a non stick and toss the pasta in it. Sprinkle a pinch of salt and some pepper on it and mix till it's heated. Remove from fire.
4. Heat the prepared tomato sauce. Add pasta and heat through. Transfer to a serving dish.
5. Serve sprinkled with grated cheese and basil leaves.

Fettuccine Primavera

Flat ribbon pasta in a cream based cheese sauce.

Serves 2-3

100 gm Fettuccine (flat ribbon pasta) - boiled (2-2½ cups)
3 tbsp olive oil or 2 tbsp butter
3-4 flakes garlic - crushed
75 gm mushrooms - cut into thin slices
2 spring onions - cut diagonally into slices
1 red or green or yellow capsicum - cut into four and then cut widthwise into thin pieces
5-6 baby corns - cut into diagonal slices of about ¼" thickness
½ cup cream
½ cup grated cheese, preferably mozzarella
¼ tsp pepper
¼ tsp red chilli flakes
salt to taste

1. Boil 4 cups of water with 1 tsp salt. When the water starts to boil, gradually slide in the fettuccine from the side of the pan. Stir well. Boil for about 4-5 minutes till done.
2. While the fettuccine is boiling, heat olive oil or butter in a pan or kadhai.
3. Add garlic. Stir for a few seconds. Add mushroom slices. Cook for 1-2 minutes on high flame.
4. Add spring onions, baby corns and capsicum and stir fry for 1 minute.
5. Add salt, pepper and chilli flakes.
6. Reduce heat and add the cream. Bring to a boil on low heat.
7. Add cheese, leaving aside some for the top. Mix well till smooth. Remove from fire. Keep sauce aside.
8. Drain the fettuccine and refresh under cold water. Add to the hot sauce and stir well to coat nicely in cream sauce.
9. Serve immediately, sprinkled with some cheese. If you want to serve later, always remember to cover when heating the pasta as the edges of the pasta tend to turn hard if not covered.

Stuffed Cheese Steaks with Salsa

Serves 4   *Picture on page 127*

400 gm cottage cheese (paneer) - cut into 1½"x 2" squares of ¾" thickness

FILLING
½ cube cheese - grated finely (2 tbsp)
6-7 french beans - cut into paper thin slices, ¼ cup finely grated carrot (½ carrot)
¼ tsp salt, ¼ tsp oregano, a pinch of pepper, or to taste
½ tbsp butter, 1 tbsp grated onion (½ onion)

BATTER
3 tbsp plain flour (maida), ¼ cup plus 1 tbsp milk
2 pinches of turmeric (haldi), ¼ tsp salt, ¼ tsp red chilli powder
2 tbsp very finely grated cheese

SALSA
5 tomatoes - roasted, 2 onion - chopped finely
2 green chillies - chopped, 2 tbsp chopped coriander
1 tbsp oil, 1 tsp vinegar, ½ tsp salt and ¼ tsp pepper, or to taste

1. Cut cottage cheese into thick, big rectangular pieces. Divide each piece into 2 pieces. Sprinkle salt and freshly ground pepper on both sides on each piece.
2. For the filling, heat butter. Add onion. Stir fry for 2 minutes. Add beans. Cook covered for 3 minutes on low heat till soft. Add carrots, salt, pepper, oregano, grated cheese and stir for 1 minute. Remove from fire and keep aside to cool. .
3. Take a piece of cottage cheese. Spread 1 tsp of the filling on it. Press another piece of cottage cheese on it. Turn and press the other side also. Keep aside.
4. For the batter, mix all ingredients of the batter together.
5. To prepare the salsa, pierce a tomato with a fork and hold it over the naked flame to roast it till the skin turns blackish and charred. Roast all the tomatoes like this. Cool and peel. Chop 2 tomatoes and puree the other 3 tomatoes. Heat oil and saute onion and green chillies till onion turns soft. Add all other ingredients and cook for just 1 minute. Do not cook further. Remove from fire. Keep aside.
6. At serving time heat ½ tbsp butter in a pan on medium heat. Dip the stuffed steak in the prepare batter to coat all sides and put in the pan. Cook 4 pieces at a time. Reduce heat after 2 minutes when the edges start changing colour. Turn the side gently with a knife or a flat spoon. Cook till browned on both sides.
7. Serve hot with salsa, mustard sauce and boiled vegetables.

Broccoli Macaroni Italiano

Serves 2-3

1 cup uncooked macaroni

SAUCE
3 tbsp olive oil or 2 tbsp butter
1 tbsp garlic - crushed
1 medium head (150-200 gm) broccoli - cut into medium florets
4-5 (50 gm) baby corns - cut into ¼" thick round slices (½ cup)
3 tomatoes - chopped very finely
2 tbsp tomato puree
1 tbsp tomato ketchup
¼ cup thin cream or milk
½ tsp each of oregano & red chilli flakes, 1 tsp salt, or to taste
50 gm cheese, preferably mozzarella cheese

1. Boil 5 cups of water with 1 tsp salt and 1 tsp oil. Add macaroni to boiling water. Boil for 5 minutes or till almost done. Leave in hot water for a 2-3 minutes to get completely done. Strain and refresh in cold water.
2. While the macaroni is boiling, crush and chop garlic, cut broccoli into florets and baby corn into small round pieces. Keep aside.
3. Heat oil or butter in a kadhai or a non stick pan, add garlic, stir.
4. Add the broccoli. Stir for a minute. Cover on low heat for 2-3 minutes till tender, but firm.
5. Add baby corns and stir for 2 minutes.
6. Add tomatoes and cook till tomatoes turn soft.
7. Add tomato puree, tomato ketchup, oregano, chill flakes and salt. Mix.
8. Add macaroni. Stir gently till macaroni is well coated.
9. Add cream or milk. Pour into a serving dish and garnish with grated cheese.

Note: As macaroni absorbs moisture, the sauce should be slightly thin to coat the macaroni well. The macaroni should only be added at the time of serving. You may use paneer instead of baby corns. Cut paneer into small pieces and add at step 8 along with the boiled macaroni.

Mushrooms in Lemon Cream Sauce

Serves 3-4

200 gm mushrooms - sliced thickly
2 tbsp butter
2 tbsp olive oil or any cooking oil
2-3 flakes garlic - minced

MIX TOGETHER IN A BOWL
1½ tbsp lemon juice
1 tsp tomato ketchup
½ cup fresh cream
2 tbsp finely sliced chives or spring onion greens or chopped parsley
½ tsp salt and ½ tsp freshly ground pepper, or to taste
1 tsp cornflour
½ cup water

1. Heat the butter and oil in a pan add the garlic and cook for 1 minute.
2. Add the mushrooms and cook for 3-4 minutes, till golden. Remove from fire. Keep aside in the pan till the time of serving.
3. Mix all ingredients together in a bowl and keep in the refrigerator till the time of serving.
4. At the time of serving, add the mixed ingredients in the bowl to the mushrooms in the pan. Mix well. Keep the pan on fire and bring to a boil, stirring constantly. Cook for 1 minute until a sauce is ready.
5. Serve hot with garlic bread cut into slices, drizzled with oil and made crisp golden in the oven.

Corn Lasagne

A lighter version of the traditional dish, this recipe does not have the heavy sauce. You might like to use paneer in place of Tofu in the recipe. You may use any long, flat pasta instead of lasagne.

Serves 6

3 sheets lasagne
150 gm tofu or paneer - grated and sprinkled with some salt and pepper
1 cup grated cheese, preferably mozzarella

FILLING
2 tbsp olive oil or any other cooking oil
¼ cup grated cabbage, ¼ cup finely chopped carrot
½ red and ½ green capsicum or 1 green capsicum - finely chopped
½ cup sweet corn kernels (tinned) - drained
3 large tomatoes - blanched and mashed
2 tbsp ready made tomato puree
3 tbsp fresh basil - chopped or 1 tsp dried basil
¾ tsp salt and ¼ tsp freshly ground black pepper, ½ tsp sugar, or to taste

1. Boil 6 cups of water in a large pan with 2 tsp salt and 1 tbsp oil. Add lasagne sheets to boiling water, one at a time, and boil till soft. (about 5 minutes.) Remove from water and place them separately on a flat surface.
2. Add tomatoes to boiling water and boil for 3 minutes. Remove from water. Cool and peel the skin. Mash the tomatoes.
3. To make filling, heat oil in a pan, add cabbage, carrot, capsicum, corn, mashed tomatoes, tomato puree and basil. Cook over a medium heat, stirring frequently, until boiling. Reduce heat and simmer covered for 15 minutes or until vegetables are soft and mixture reduces and thickens. Add salt, sugar and pepper to taste. Keep filling aside.
4. Divide filling and paneer — both into three portions.
5. Spread 1/3 of filling in a lightly greased oven proof dish.
6. Cover with a layer of lasagne sheet and spread with 1/3 of the paneer and then filling.
7. Repeat layers — lasagne sheet, half of the paneer, filling, lasagne and last portion of paneer. Cover the last sheet nicely with paneer.
8. Sprinkle grated cheese to cover nicely and bake in a moderately hot oven at 180°C for 20 minutes or until lasagne sheets are tender.

Penne in Cream Sauce

Pasta with baby corns in a white, creamy cheese sauce.

Serves 4

2 cups uncooked penne pasta - boiled
1 tsp oregano
200 gm baby corns - sliced (1½ cups)
4 tbsp butter
4 flakes garlic - crushed
2 tbsp maida (plain flour)
1 tbsp chopped parsley or coriander
1½ cups milk
½ cup fresh cream (100 gm)
100 gm (1 cup grated) mozzarella cheese
salt to taste, a few black peppercorns (saboot kali mirch) - roughly powdered

GARNISH
2-3 black olives - sliced, chopped parsley

1. Melt 3 tbsp butter. Add sliced baby corns and saute for 4-5 minutes.
2. Reduce heat. Add garlic. Stir for a few seconds.
3. Add flour. Cook on low heat for 1 minute.
4. Add parsley or coriander.
5. Remove from fire. Add milk, mix well to dissolve the flour. See that there are no lumps. Return to heat. Boil. Cook for 2 minutes, till it starts coating the spoon and turns a little thick. Remove from heat.
6. Add ½ cup cheese and cream. Add salt to taste. Keep sauce aside till the time of serving.
7. At the time of serving, heat 1 tbsp butter in a large non stick pan or kadhai and toss the pasta in it till it gets heated. Add oregano and ½ tsp salt, or to taste. Mix and remove from fire.
8. To serve, spread warm pasta on a plate. To heat sauce, keep on low heat and remove from fire when it is just about to boil. Pour hot sauce over the pasta. Sprinkle remaining cheese and crushed peppercorns. Serve garnished with black olives and parsley.

RICE & BREADS

Quick Mexican Rice

Serves 3-4

1 cup rice - soaked for 1 hour
2 tbsp oil, ¼ tsp jeera (cumin seeds)
1" stick dalchini (cinnamon), 1 moti illaichi (black cardamom)
¼ cup nutri nugget granules - soaked in water for ½ hour
1 cup tomato puree
½ tsp salt, ¼ tsp red chilli powder
1 big onion - sliced, for garnishing

1. Heat oil in a pressure cooker. Add onions and fry till well browned. Remove from cooker and keep aside for garnishing.
2. In the same oil, add jeera, dalchini and moti illaichi. Let jeera turn brown.
3. Drain the nutri nugget granules. Squeeze and wash them well. Add them to the cooker and fry on low heat for 2-3 minutes.
4. Add ¼ cup water and pressure cook to give 1 whistle. After the pressure drops, add the drained rice to the nugget mixture along with salt, chilli powder and tomato puree. Mix gently.
5. Pressure cook on high heat. Remove from fire when it is just about to give a whistle. Do not let the whistle come. Garnish with fried onions. Serve.

Garlic Bread

Serves 4-6

long garlic bread loaf - cut diagonally into ¼" thick slices
2-3 tbsp butter
1 tsp basil (dried) or oregano or ½ tsp freshly crushed pepper
2 flakes garlic - crushed
75 gm pizza cheese (mozzarella) - grated
2-3 tbsp olive oil

1. Cut the garlic bread into moderately thick slices diagonally.
2. Mix the butter, basil and garlic.
3. Apply this butter lightly on the bread slice.
4. Sprinkle grated cheese on them. Pour some olive oil on the cheese.
5. Heat oven to 210°C. Place on the grill rack of the oven and grill the slices (10 minutes) till slightly crisp and toasted. Serve hot.

Zafrani Pullao

Picture on facing page   Serves 3-4

1 cup basmati rice - wash in 2-3 changes of water. Strain and let the rice be in the strainer for 30 minutes (do not soak)
¼ tsp kesar (saffron) - soak in 2 tbsp warm water
4 tbsp oil, ½ tsp shah jeera (black cumin)
1 onion - cut into slices
8-10 almonds, 1 tbsp kishmish
1 carrot - cut into round slices
¼ of a small cauliflower - cut into small florets
10 french beans - cut into ½" pieces
½ cup leaves of poodina (mint)
1½ tsp salt, ½ tsp haldi, 1 tbsp lemon juice

PASTE (GRIND WITH A LITTLE WATER)
4 flakes garlic, ½" piece ginger
seeds of 4 chhoti illaichi (green cardamoms), 1 moti illaichi (black cardamom)
2 laung, 2-3 saboot kali mirch, ½" piece dalchini (cinnamon)
½ tsp jeera (cumin seeds)

1. Wash and strain rice. Let it be in the strainer for 30 minutes.
2. Grind all ingredients of the paste together with a little water to a paste. Keep this ginger-garlic-spice paste aside.
3. Heat oil in a heavy bottomed pan. Add shah jeera. Wait for 1 minute till jeera crackles.
4. Add onion slices and stir till light brown.
5. Add almonds and kishmish. Saute for a few seconds.
6. Add all vegetables. Stir for 2-3 minutes.
7. Add the freshly ground ginger-garlic-spice paste and salt. Stir to mix well. Bhuno vegetables for 2 minutes with this paste.
8. Add rice.
9. Add the soaked kesar. Do not mix.
10. Add 2 cups warm water and poodina leaves. Boil.
11. Add haldi. Stir to mix. Reduce heat and cook covered till the water dries up, for about 14-15 minutes.
12. Serve rice with any raita of your choice.

Mushroom Dinner Rolls

It makes a complete meal with a baked dish or pasta.

Serves 6-8

6-8 small dinner rolls (small buns)
1-2 tbsp melted butter

FILLING
100 gm mushrooms - cut into small thin slices
1½ tbsp butter, 1 tbsp maida
¾ cup milk
1 green chilli - chopped or ½ capsicum - chopped
2 tbsp chopped coriander, salt & pepper to taste

TOPPING
25 gm (1 cube) cheese - grated
red chilli flakes and prepared English mustard

1. Heat oven to 210°C.
2. Cut a thin slice from the top of the dinner roll and with the back of a spoon, scoop out the centre, leaving a thick shell all around, to get a small hollow. Brush the scooped hollow and the out sides with melted butter. Place on a grill tray. Grill for 5 minutes at 210°C or till crisp.
3. Meanwhile prepare the filling: heat ½ tbsp butter in a kadhai or non stick pan and add the mushrooms and saute for 1 minute. Remove on to a plate. In the same sauce pan add 1 tbsp of butter and add the flour. Cook till slightly brown, lower heat and add the milk. Cook till quite thick. Add the mushrooms, green chilli or capsicum, coriander or parsley, salt and pepper to taste. Remove from heat.
4. Remove the crisp buns from the oven and spoon some filling in hollow or scooped portion.
5. Sprinkle cheese and return to the oven for 2 minutes or till cheese melts. Sprinkle chilli flakes and dot with mustard. Serve with a hearty soup and a baked dish to make up a complete meal.

Broccoli & Carrot Rice

Serves 4

1 cup uncooked Basmati rice - soaked for 1 hour
1½ cups medium sized florets of broccoli
1 carrot - cut into cubes
3 tbsp oil
½ tsp jeera
¼ tsp saboot kali mirch (pepper corns)
1 onion - sliced finely
1¼ tsp salt or to taste

1. Boil 2 cups water with 1 tsp salt and 1 tsp sugar Add florets of broccoli and carrot cubes.
2. Reduce flame and simmer for 2 minutes.
3. Drain & keep aside.
4. Heat oil. Add jeera and saboot kali mirch.
5. When jeera changes colour, add onions. Stir fry till transparent.
6. Add broccoli and carrots. Stir fry on low flame for 2 minutes.
7. Add rice. Stir fry gently for ½ a minute.
8. Add 2 cups water. Mix.
9. When the rice boils, reduce flame. Cover it with a towel napkin and then with a tight fitting lid.
10. Cook on very low flame till rice is done and the water absorbed.

Vegetable Risotto

Serves 6-8

2 cups uncooked rice - washed and kept in the strainer for 1 hour
2 onions - chopped finely
15-20 french beans - threaded and cut into small cubes
1 carrot - cut into small cubes
4 tbsp readymade tomato puree
1 tsp sugar
50 gm cheese - grated
3 tbsp butter
3 tsp salt or to taste
1 tsp pepper

1. Chop the onions finely.
2. Cut the carrots and french beans into small cubes.
3. Heat the butter in a heavy bottomed pan and fry the onions till transparent.
4. Add vegetables and stir fry for 2-3 minutes.
5. Add rice and tomato puree. Stir fry gently on low heat for 2-3 minutes till the rice gets well fried.
6. Add 4 cups water. Add sugar, salt & pepper. Keep on low flame for 10-12 minutes.
7. When the rice is almost cooked, sprinkle cheese all over on the rice. Do not stir. Cover and cook for a few minutes till the rice is fully cooked.
   The cheese melts and goes into the rice.
8. Sprinkle some cheese on top at the time of serving. Serve hot.

Nan Badaami

Makes 6

2½ cups (250 gm) maida (plain flour)
½ cup hot milk
1 tsp baking powder
½ cup warm water (approx.)
½ tsp salt
10 badaam (almonds) - cut into long thin pieces (slivered)

1. Heat milk and put it in a paraat (large pan). Add baking powder to the hot milk. Mix well and keep it aside for 1-2 minutes.
2. Sift maida and salt together. Add maida to the hot milk. Mix.
3. Knead to a dough with enough warm water.
4. Keep in a warm place for 3-4 hours.
5. Make 6-8 balls.
6. Roll out each ball to an oblong shape. Spread ghee all over. Fold one side (lengthways) a little, so as to overlap an inch of the nan. Press on the joint with the belan (rolling pin).
7. Sprinkle some chopped almonds. Press with a rolling pin (belan). Pull one side of the nan to give it a pointed end like the shape of the nan.
8. Apply some water on the back side of the nan. Stick in a hot tandoor.
9. Cook till nan is ready. Spread butter on the ready nan and serve hot.

Mushroom-Parsley Bruschetta

Hot & crisp garlic flavoured bread pieces topped with herbed mushrooms.

Makes 20 pieces

TOPPING
200 gm mushrooms - chopped finely, ¾ cup chopped fresh parsley
4 tbsp oil
1 big onion - chopped very finely, 4 flakes garlic - chopped very finely
1 tsp dried oregano, ¾ tsp salt & ½ tsp freshly ground peppercorns, or to taste

BREAD
a small French bread - cut into slices of ½" thickness, about 18-20 slices
4 tbsp olive oil, 4 flakes garlic - crushed

1. Heat oil. Add garlic and onions. Cook for 2 minutes till onions are golden.
2. Add mushrooms and cook for 2-3 minutes. Add parsley.
3. Add salt, pepper and oregano and mix well. Remove from fire.
4. For the bread, mix 2-3 crushed garlic flakes with 2 tbsp olive oil.
5. Spoon ¼ tsp of this flavoured oil on each slice and spread it on the slice with the back of the spoon. Keep aside till serving time.
6. At serving time, bake the bread slices in a preheated oven at 200°C/360°F for 10 minutes till each is lightly toasted and crisp. Alternately, toast the slices on a pan or tawa on low heat till crisp on both sides.
7. Spread 1 heaped tbsp of mushroom mixture (at room temperature) on the toasted slice. Serve immediately.

Tandoori Roti

Makes 6-7

2 ½ cups atta (whole wheat flour)
1 cup water (approx.)
½ tsp salt
2-3 tbsp ghee

1. Keep ghee in the fridge for some time, so that it solidifies.
2. Make a soft dough with atta, salt and water. Keep aside for half an hour.
3. Divide the dough into 6 equal balls. Flatten each ball, roll out each into a round of 5" diameter.
4. Spread 1 tsp of solidified ghee. Sprinkle a teaspoon of dry flour on the ghee.
5. Make a slit, starting from any one end till almost to the other end, leaving just 1".
6. Start rolling from the slit, to form an even cone. Roll out, to a diameter of 5", applying pressure only at the centre and not on the sides.
7. Cook carefully in a heated tandoor till brown specs appear.

Jeera Parantha

Makes 8

2 cups atta (whole wheat flour)
1 tbsp roasted jeera (bhuna jeera)
½ tsp ajwain (carom seeds)
2 tbsp ghee
½ tsp salt, ½ tsp red chilli powder

1. Mix atta with ajwain, 1 tbsp ghee, salt, chilli powder and ½ of the jeera. Add enough water to make a dough of rolling consistency. Cover and keep the dough aside for 30 minutes.
2. Make walnut sized balls. Roll out a little to make a thick chappati.
3. Spread 1 tsp ghee all over. Fold a little from the left and then right to meet in the centre. Fold the top and the bottom to now get a square.
4. Roll out to get a square parantha, but do not make it too thin. Sprinkle little jeera. Press with the belan (rolling pin).
5. Cook on a tawa, frying on both sides till crisp and well browned.

Quick Peethi Poori

Makes 12

1 cup atta (whole wheat flour)
1 tsp oil or melted ghee, ½ tsp salt
¼ cup urad dal - soaked for 2 hours and coarsely ground to get peethi
or ½ cup ready made dal ki peethi
½ tsp salt, 1 tsp kuti laal mirch (red chilli flakes), ¼ tsp ajwain (carom seeds)

1. Sift flour and ½ tsp salt together and rub in melted ghee or oil.
2. Knead to a little stiff dough with about ¾-1 cup water and set aside.
3. Mix dal ki peethi with ½ tsp salt, 1 tsp kuti laal mirch and ¼ tsp ajwain.
4. Divide dough into small balls and roll out the balls into small poories.
5. Spread 1 tsp full peethi on the rolled out poori with the spoon.
6. Heat oil, drop the rolled poories gently into it with the peethi side down in the oil, so that the dal gets cooked in the hot oil.
7. Press the sides of the poori with a perforated frying spoon and make the poori swell up. Turn. Fry till golden brown. Drain on brown paper.

Note: The peethi can be stuffed inside the poori also, but the above method is quicker!

Poodina Parantha

Makes 6

2 cups atta (whole wheat flour)
4 tbsp freshly chopped or dry poodina (mint leaves)
1 tsp ajwain (carom seeds)
2 tbsp oil, ½ tsp salt
½ tsp red chilli powder

1. Mix atta with all ingredients except poodina. Add enough water to make a dough of rolling consistency.
2. Make walnut sized balls. Flatten to make a thick chappati.
3. Spread 1 tsp of ghee all over. Cut a slit from the outer edge till the centre. Start rolling from the slit to form a cone. Press cone gently.
4. Roll out. Sprinkle poodina. Press with the belan (rolling pin).
5. Cook on a tawa, frying on both sides or apply some water on the back side of the parantha and stick it in a hot tandoor. Serve hot.

Southern Curd Rice

A perfect dish during the scorching heat of summers.

Serves 4 *Picture on page 117*

4 cups cooked rice
1 cup milk
1 cup fresh curd - beaten
1 tsp salt, or to taste
2 tbsp ghee or 3-4 tbsp oil
1 tbsp channa dal
1 tbsp urad dal
1 tsp sarson (mustard seeds)
1 tsp jeera (cumin seeds)
2 dry, red chillies - broken into small pieces
2-3 tbsp chopped ginger
10-15 curry leaves

1. Place the cooked rice (boil it in water and drain the water) in a bowl.
2. Soak the rice with milk.
3. Beat the curd with salt and add to the rice. Keep aside.
4. To temper the rice, heat ghee or oil in a pan or kadhai. Add dals and stir on low heat till they slightly change colour. Add the sarson and jeera. When jeera turns golden, add ginger and red chillies. Stir for 1 minute. Add curry patta. Remove from fire.
5. Add the curd-rice mixture into the tempered oil and mix gently.
6. Transfer to a serving dish. Keep at room temperature for 1 hour and then refrigerate or serve at room temperature.
7. Serve with lemon pickle and fried papad.

DESSERTS

Water Melon Curry : Recipe on page 49 ➤
Southern Curd Rice : Recipe on page 115 ➤

Glazed Grape Mousse

Servings 8

½ tin milk-maid (condensed milk)
250 gm black grapes (2 cups)
2 tbsp sugar
300 gm cream
4 tsp gelatine

GLAZE
1 tsp gelatine - soaked in ¼ cup water
½ cup black grapes
2 tbsp sugar
½ tsp cornflour - dissolved in 2 tbsp water

1. Cook grapes with 1¼ cups water and 2 tbsp sugar. Boil. Keep boiling on low heat for 10 minutes till syrupy. Remove from fire. Cool. Blend in a mixer for a few seconds till pulpy. Keep grape puree aside.
2. Mix gelatine in ½ cup water. Heat on slow fire till it dissolves.
3. Add gelatine to the grape puree.
4. Beat condensed milk in a pan till creamy. Add grape puree. Mix well.
5. Chill in the freezer till the mixture is slightly thick.
6. Whip 250 gms cream till slightly thick.
7. Beat the thickened grape mixture also till smooth.
8. Add whipped cream to grape mixture.
9. Transfer to a serving dish or individual cups. Keep in the fridge to set.
10. To prepare the glaze, soak 1 tsp gelatine in ¼ cup water. Cook ½ cup grapes with ¼ cup water and 2 tbsp sugar. Boil. Mash and cook till pulpy for about 3-5 minutes. Add ½ tsp cornflour dissolved in 2 tbsp water. Cook till thick and saucy. Add the gelatine and cook for 1 minute on low heat. Remove from fire and bring down to room temperature.
11. Pour the sauce over the mousse. Keep it in the refrigerator to set.
12. Whip 50 gm of cream till stiff. Pipe a star on the mousse. Top it with a grape.

Creamy Lemon Dessert

Serves 4-5

250 gm (1¼ cups) fresh cream
½ tin (¾ cup) condensed milk - cold
¼ cup lemon juice (juice of 4 lemons)
rind (peel) of 1 lemon, a pinch or a few drops yellow colour

CRUST
1 packet (10) good day biscuits
4 tbsp (50 gm) melted butter

1. Keep the cream in a bowl and chill for 10 minutes in the freezer.
2. To prepare the crust, preheat oven to 180°C. Break good day biscuits into pieces and put in a polythene. Crush to a coarse powder with a belan (rolling pin). Do not make them too fine. Put them in a bowl.
3. Melt butter and add 4 tbsp melted butter to the biscuit crumbs. Mix well.
4. Spread crumbs in the serving dish, (a small square borosil dish in fine). Press well. Bake at 180°C for 10 minutes. Remove from oven and cool.
5. While the crust is being baked, wash & grate 1 lemon with the peel gently on the grater to get lemon rind. Do not apply pressure and see that the white pith beneath the lemon peel is not grated along with the yellow rind.
6. Take out ¼ cup lemon juice. Add the rind to it.
7. Empty ½ tin of cold condensed milk (keep condensed milk in fridge) into a bowl. Add lemon juice and beat well. The condensed milk turns thick on whipping. Keep in the fridge.
8. Beat chilled cream in the chilled bowl with an electric egg beater (hand.mixer) till soft peaks are formed. After soft peaks are ready, beat gently with a spoon till firm peaks are formed. Beat carefully in a cool place or over ice, taking care not to beat vigorously. The cream should remain smooth and not turn buttery or granular. Put about ½ cup cream in an icing bag for decoration and keep in the fridge.
9. Add half of the thickened condensed milk to the cream in the bowl. Fold condensed milk gently into the cream to mix well. Fold in the left over condensed milk too. Add enough colour to get a nice yellow colour.
10. Pour the cream mix over the cooled biscuit crust in the dish. Keep in the fridge for atleast 3 hours to set and if you want to serve soon, chill in the freezer compartment for ½ to 1 hour. To serve, cut into squares.

Quick Tiramisu

An Italian favourite!

Picture on page 1

Serves 5-6

400 gm (2 cups) fresh cream - cold
2 tbsp cheese spread
1 tsp vanilla essence
¾ cup powdered sugar
1 tbsp rum or brandy (optional)
2-3 tbsp cocoa to sprinkle

ESPRESSO COFFEE (½ CUP)
¼ cup water, ½ cup milk
1 tsp coffee, 2 tsp sugar

CHOCOLATE CHIP BISCUITS (4 PACKS)

1. Chill cream in a beating bowl in the freezer for 10 minutes. Chill the blades of the beater or the wire whisk also.
2. Beat cheese spread with sugar with an electric egg beater, till smooth.
3. Add the cream, essence and brandy. Beat till thick. Beat over ice or in a cool room during the hot weather.
4. After it turns thick, gently beat till soft peaks form, preferably with a tablespoon and not an electric egg beater. Do not over beat. If the cream starts looking granular, immediately stop beating. Put whipped cream in the freezer for a few minutes.
5. To prepare espresso coffee boil water and milk together. Simmer for a minute. Add sugar. Mix. Remove from fire. Add coffee and mix well. Cool to room temperature.
6. Soak biscuits in coffee and arrange biscuits at the bottom of a small rectangular borosil dish. Soak some more biscuits and place them on the biscuits in the dish to get a thick layer of biscuits. (Use 2 packs of biscuits for each layer).
7. Spread ½ of the whipped cream mixture. Level it gently.
8. Again put a layer of soaked biscuits making the layer thick by using 2 packs of biscuits.
9. Spread the remaining cream and level gently. Chill in the freezer for 10 minutes.
10. Sift 2 tbsp cocoa through a strainer over the dessert. Make squares using a toothpick as shown in the picture. Cover with a cling film and refrigerate for atleast 1-2 hours till well set. Cut into squares to serve.

Ice cream Trifle

Serves 8

3-4 black forest pastries or any other pastries
1 tin mixed tinned fruit or 2 cups chopped fresh fruits
1 family pack (500 ml) vanilla ice cream
1-2 tbsp chocolate sauce to top
a few almonds - cut into thin long pieces

1. Cut the pastries into 3 slices. (Open the layers of the pastry). Place them in a shallow serving dish covering the bottom of the dish.
2. Take a knife and spread the cream of the top layer evenly on the pastries.
3. Soak the pastries with 4-5 tbsp of the mixed fruit syrup (should feel slightly moist). If using fresh fruit, soak the pastries with cold milk.
4. Spread the drained, canned fruit or chopped fresh fruit on the pastries.
5. At serving time, top the fruit with scoops of ice cream.
6. Pour a few swirls of chocolate sauce on the ice cream.
7. Decorate with some almonds and serve.

Strawberry Cheese Cake

Serves 8-10

2½ cups thick curd - hang for ½ hour
250 gm (1½ cups) fresh cream, 2 tbsp cheese spread, 7 tbsp powdered sugar
½ cup strawberry crush or fresh puree of strawberries
4 level tsp gelatine mixed in ¼ cup water
some strawberries or tinned cherries

BASE
a sponge cake, 4-5 tbsp strawberry crush or jam - beat well to make it smooth
2-3 tbsp cold milk

GARNISH
whipped cream
fresh strawberries or tinned cherries, a few almonds, mint leaves

1. Soak gelatine in ¼ cup water for 5 minutes. Heat on very low flame to dissolve the gelatine. Keep aside.
2. Beat cream with sugar till slightly fluffy but still thin.
3. Beat hung curd till smooth. Add cheese spread and whip till smooth.
4. Add gelatine solution. Mix well.
5. Mix the whipped cream and curd mixture.
6. Add strawberry crush and mix well to get a bright pink colour. Check sugar, add more if required, depending on the sourness of the curd.
7. Chill in the freezer for 10 minutes, or till slightly thick, but do not let it set.
8. Meanwhile, cut a ½" thick slice from the bottom of the sponge cake. Cover the bottom of a loose bottomed flan tin, such as to cover the base. Press well.
9. Sprinkle some cold milk on the cake. Spread 3-4 tbsp crush or jam and keep in the fridge to chill.
10. When the curd-cream mixture becomes slightly thick, beat it till smooth and pour over the cake in the flan tin. Chill in the fridge for at least 4-6 hours, till well set. Serve garnished with whipped cream, fresh strawberries or cherries, mint leaves and almonds.

Note: Left over cake can be made into trifle pudding with some custard & fruits or a fruit gateau - a cake layered with whipped cream & fruits.

Lychee Pearls

A very decorative & a delicious dessert with an Indian flavour. Assure your guests that the seed of the fruit has been removed and replaced with a blanched almond to enjoy the fruit comfortably.

Serves 8-10   *Picture on page 51*

20-25 large lychees
20-25 almonds - blanched (soaked in hot water and skin removed)
10 sheets of warq (silver sheets)
½ tin of milk maid (condensed milk) (3/4 cup)
½ cup of milk
250 gm paneer - grated
¼ tsp kesar (saffron) - soaked in 1 tbsp rose water
300 gm cream - chilled nicely and whipped till it turns thick

GARNISH
a few rose petals
a few green pistas - sliced

1. Peel and carefully deseed the lychees, keeping the lychees whole.
2. Insert one almond in each lychee in place of the seed.
3. Open up a varak carefully. Place 2 lychees with the broad end (open end) downwards on the sheet leaving some space in-between the two lychees. Carefully lift the paper beneath the varak to coat the lychees with varak. Do not touch the varak directly. Keep the pearl lychees covered in a plate and refrigerate.
4. Soak the saffron in rose water.
5. Whip the chilled cream (chill the cream before whipping) till slightly thick.
6. Beat ½ tin condensed milk, ½ cup milk and saffron along with the rose water in a pan till smooth.
7. Add the grated paneer and mix well.
8. Add cream to the condensed milk mixture to get a kheer like consistency of the mixture (thick pouring consistency). If you like it less sweet, add some more grated paneer.
9. Transfer to a shallow serving dish. Top the milk maid mixture with pearl lychees. Garnish with rose petals and sliced pistas. Serve chilled.

Baked Pineapple
with Fruity Caramel Sauce

Enjoy it by itself or topped with some ice cream.

Serves 5-6

1 fresh, ripe pineapple
1 tbsp salted butter
3 tbsp sugar

BLEND TOGETHER
1 large mango - peeled and chopped
1 banana
½" piece soft ginger - grated

OTHER INGREDIENTS
½ cup sugar - to caramelize
½ of a family pack of vanilla ice cream
10 almonds - cut into thin long pieces, for decoration

1. Peel the pineapple and cut into rings of ¼-½" thickness. Cut ring into 2 pieces and remove the hard core. Chop into 1" pieces. Heat 1 tbsp butter in a pan. Add pineapple and 2 tbsp sugar. Mix well for a few seconds only to coat them with butter. Remove from fire.
2. Place the buttered pineapple in a shallow oven-proof dish. Sprinkle 1 tbsp sugar over it. Heat oven to 175°C and place the pineapple in it and bake for 25-30 minutes. Remove from oven.
3. To prepare the sauce, place peeled and chopped mango, peeled banana and grated ginger in a blender and blend to a smooth puree. Keep aside. (The puree should be 1½ large cups).
4. For the sauce, heat a thick bottomed kadhai. Add ½ cup sugar. Stir on low heat till the sugar turns golden yellow in colour (like honey colour). Do not over cook or bring to a boil, it will make the sauce dark and bitter. Keeping the heat low, quickly add the pureed fruit and stir continuously for a few minutes till the puree blends well with caramel. Remove from heat.
5. Pour the fruity caramel sauce over the baked pineapples. Sprinkle almonds. Bake again at 175°C for 10-15 minutes. Remove. Serve warm or cold, topped with scoops of vanilla ice cream.

Exotic Watermelon Sauce with Ice Cream

Serves 8

1 small (2 kg approx.) watermelon (tarbooz)
1 litre vanilla ice cream

SAUCE
3 cups watermelon puree
1 tbsp cornflour
1 tbsp butter
½ cup strawberry crush
2 tbsp mixed nuts

1. Cut the watermelon, deseed it. Cut ¾ of the watermelon into neat ½" squares or make balls with a scoop. Freeze them in the freezer.
2. Puree the remaining watermelon in a blender to get about 3 cups.
3. For the sauce, mix cornflour in ½ cup puree and add to the rest of the puree. Cook on medium heat till thick. Remove from fire. Cool and add strawberry crush.
4. At the time of serving, spread ¼ of the sauce in a platter. Arrange scoops of ice cream on it. Fill the platter with frozen watermelon balls.
5. Pour the watermelon sauce over the ice cream scoops. Top with nuts. Garnish with mint leaves. Serve immediately.

Chocolate Desire

Picture on facing page   *Serves 10*

EGGLESS CHOCOLATE CAKE
1 cup maida (flour), ½ cup cornflour, ¼ cup cocoa
1½ tsp baking powder, ¾ tsp soda-bi-carb
¾ cup butter (75-80 gm), ¾ cup powdered sugar
1 cup milk, ½ tsp vanilla essence
20 gm dark chocolate or milk chocolate mixed with 4 tbsp milk

TO SOAK
¼ cup milk, 1 tsp sugar, ½ tsp vanilla essence

FILLING ICING
150 gm fresh cream, 3 tbsp powdered sugar, 3-4 tbsp cocoa powder
1 tbsp almonds - crushed

TOP ICING
50 gm fresh cream, 2 slabs of dark chocolate (80 gm) - cut into small pieces

1. For the cake, sift flour, cornflour, cocoa, baking powder and soda-bi-carb.
2. Beat butter and sugar till fluffy. Add flour and 1 cup milk. Mix well.
3. Cut chocolate into small pieces. Melt with 4 tbsp milk in a heavy bottomed kadhai on very low heat. Add melted chocolate and essence to the cake batter.
4. Beat till fluffy. Bake in a greased 8" diameter cake tin at 180°C for 30-35 minutes. If a knife inserted in the centre of the cake comes out clean, remove from oven.
5. Cool the cake. Cut through the cake, horizontally into 2 round pieces.
6. Mix ¼ cup of cold milk with 1 tsp sugar and essence. Soak each piece of cake with 2-3 tbsp of this milk. Keep aside to cool.
7. For the filling, mix cocoa powder in ½ cup cream till well mixed. Add to the rest of the cream. Add sugar and beat well till stiff peaks are ready. Keep chocolate cream aside.
8. Place a piece of cake on a serving plate. Spread the chocolate cream on it.
9. Sprinkle almonds. Invert the second piece of cake on it. Press very lightly.
10. For the top icing, heat the cream in a small heavy bottom pan on low heat. (Do not boil). Add chocolate pieces and stir continuously till chocolate melts and becomes a smooth paste. Immediately pour over the cake and tilt the cake to cover the cake completely. Keep in the fridge for 30 minutes for the icing to set.

Stuffed Cheese Steaks with Salsa : Recipe on page 99, Chocolate Desire ➤

Nita Mehta's BEST SELLERS (Vegetarian)

BREAKFAST Non-Vegetarian

The Art of BAKING

JHATPAT KHAANA

Indian Cooking - Handi Tawa Kadhai

Different ways with CHAAWAL

PRESSURE COOKING

SOUTH INDIAN FAVOURITES

PARTY FOOD

STAY SLIM...EAT RIGHT

LOW FAT Tasty Recipes

Mocktails & Snacks

All Time Favourite SNACKS

ITALIAN Veg. Cookery

PASTA & CORN

CONTINENTAL Veg. Cookery

CHINESE Veg. Cuisine

MICROWAVE Veg. Cookery

DESSERTS & PUDDINGS

Delicious Parlour ICE CREAM

Soups Salads & Starters

DAL & ROTI

Taste of RAJASTHAN

Taste of GUJARAT

Taste of PUNJAB

NAVRATRI RECIPES

SANDWICHES

Green Vegetables

PANEER ALL THE WAY